CONTENTS

Murder
in the
Name of Allah

Murder
in the
Name of Allah

Hazrat Mirza Tahir Ahmad

Translated by

Syed Barakat Ahmad

Lutterworth Press
Cambridge

Lutterworth Press
P.O. Box 60
Cambridge CB1 2NT

British Library Cataloguing in Publication Data

Ahmad, Hazrat Mirza Tahir
  Murder in the Name of Allah.
  1. Islam
  I. Title II. Mazhab Ke nam per khoon.
  English
  297

ISBN 0-7188-28054

Printed in Great Britain by
St Edmundsbury Press Ltd., Bury St Edmunds, Suffolk

EDITOR'S FOREWORD

Hardly a day passes on which an Islamic event does not make headlines. The president of a Muslim state is assassinated by the supporters of Muslim Brotherhood; a European journalist is taken hostage by Islamic Jihad; a Pan-Am aircraft is hijacked by another Muslim group; American university professors are taken into custody by Hezbullah. The glare of 'Islamic' revolution in Iran is reflected through the flares of every Gulf oil refinery.

In 1953 there were widespread demonstrations and anti-Ahmadi riots throughout West Pakistan, leading to an almost complete breakdown of law and order. The leading trouble-makers were the Ahrar-i-Islam and the *ulema* (learned scholars), who had consistently opposed the creation of Pakistan. But it was Maulana Abul Ala Maududi, the founder of the Jamaat-e-Islami (the counterpart of the Muslim Brotherhood in Egypt), who became their voice. Martial law was proclaimed and the chief minister of the Punjab was replaced. A court of inquiry was set up jointly under Justice Mr Muhammad Munir and Justice Mr M. R. Kayani to investigate the causes of the disturbances.

No student of modern Islam should fail to read the report on the events of 1953. It explains in detail some of the problems that the new Muslim state was facing. But it is a judicial report and, as such, does not set itself the task of warning or advising. This book, however, is the work of a man of God - not simply a work written out of duty by a court official.

In 1955 Mirza Tahir Ahmad drew attention to certain aspects of the *Munir Commission Report* and spelt out the dangers the new Islamic state was facing. He showed how the Jamaat-e-Islami, despite being a minute minority of the population, would destroy Islam in Pakistan. In his book, *Mazhab ke Nam per Khoon (Murder in the Name of Religion)*, which he wrote thirty years before his election as the head of the Ahmadiyyah Movement in Islam, Mirza Tahir Ahmad shows how Islam is being exploited by the Mullahs and presented to the world as a medieval theocracy. Mirza Tahir Ahmad set the *Munir Commission Report* within the context of the Quran, *hadith* and Islamic history. He had separated fact from fiction and the law of the Quran from the interpretations of the sultan-serving *faqih*.

This slender and compact, yet challenging, book originated from *Mazhab ke Nam per Khoon*. It is written in Urdu and is addressed to educated Muslims who know both their history and the basic principles of their religion.

When I undertook the task of translating *Mazhab ke Nam per Khoon*, I had no idea whether I was biting off more than I could chew. A literal translation would be meaningless for all but experts in this field, while a translation with long, boring and distracting notes would be self-defeating. The latter would be rather like a bad tailor trying to alter a quality, made-to-measure suit for another customer - it might fit him adequately, but it would not hang as well as it would on the person for whom it was made.

This book is an updated version of *Mazhab ke Nam per Khoon* and includes some new material.

All references to important figures and events in the history of Islam which have become part of Muslim collective memory and have been mentioned by the author are fully explained. The books of tradition, Ibn Hisham's *Sirat Rasul Allah* and other primary sources have been used for this information.

Mazhab ke Nam per Khoon was a general review of the *Munir Commission Report* with special emphasis on the subject of freedom of expression in Islam. But it also discussed the brutality of the masses, the hypocrisy of the political leaders, the lack of moral courage on the part of the intellectuals and, above all, the severity of the riots, reminiscent of the events of St Bartholomew's Day (24 August 1572). This discussion has been dropped from this rendering of the text. These details are already available in the *Munir Commission Report*.

The inter-*ulema* polemics and, especially, the attacks and counterattacks of Deobandi and Brelvi supporters in the press make very interesting, but painful, reading. I have dropped them from the English version of the book, but retained a few passages to show just how low today's so-called *ulema* can stoop.

Finally, I have to admit that I have failed to convey the author's perceptive and creative imagination. I have not been able to do justice to the underlying force of his prose or the spiritual dimension of his rhetoric. Mirza Tahir Ahmad's style combines learning with humour. These qualities have been somewhat lost in translation, but I hope I have succeeded in retaining the high academic standard of the original book, which makes it a unique and inimitable work on the Islamic concept of freedom of conscience and its expression. Though I have tried my best to convey the spirit of the original - its reflective intellectuality inter-woven with the mysteries of the soul - this book remains above all a translation. Any mistakes of fact or interpretation are mine alone. If in doubt, readers should check with the original, *Mazhab ke Nam per Khoon*.

May Allah, the reader and, especially, the author forgive my short-comings.

Syed Barakat Ahmad

NOTES ON THIS TRANSLATION

References in this book to verses of the Holy Quran count the opening verse of each chapter as verse 1. Readers referring to texts which do not use this system should deduct 1 from the number quoted to arrive at the relevant verse.

The name of Muhammad, the Holy Prophet of Islam, has in general been followed by a symbol[sa] for the salutation 'may peace and blessings of Allah be upon him.' The names of other prophets and messengers of God are followed by the symbol[as], an abbreviation for 'on whom be peace'. The actual salutations have not been set out in full except in a few particular instances, in order to accommodate the text to the non-Muslim readers. They should, nevertheless, be understood as being repeated in full in each case.

In this translation the form 'ibn' has been used in both initial and medial positions in the names of persons, in order to conform with current usage, although 'bin' also occurs medially in some original texts (abbreviated usually as b.).

For the sake of consistency with quoted references, the words Mecca and Medina have been used in place of the current local transliterations of Makkah and Madinah.

INTRODUCTION

It was in the late 1950s that the original work in Urdu on which the present book is based was first undertaken. This rendering of it into English is now being offered for the benefit of English-speaking readers. The original book was published under the title *Mazhab ke Nam par Khoon*, literally translated as 'bloodshed in the name of religion'. Since then numerous editions have been printed, and it has also been translated into Bengali and Indonesian.

The main source of *Mazhab ke Nam per Khoon* was the wide-scale and most violent anti-Ahmadiyyah riots of 1953 in Pakistan. The riots were long over by the time the book was written; the wounds were almost healed, leaving some slowly fading scars behind.

But the issues those riots raised continued to live undiminished and undiluted. Is Islam a religion of war or of peace? Does Islam advocate violence, bloodshed, destruction and disorder? Does it condone persecution in any form? Does it give licence for loot, arson and murder on the pretext of doctrinal differences within Islam or *vis-à-vis* other faiths?

The book was written, therefore, not with the purpose of highlighting or resurrecting the dead and buried events of 1953, but in order to address the issues raised thereby, some of which have been mentioned above. The suffering, misery and turbulance of 1953 can be relegated to the past, of course, but the issues raised at that time continue to be of relevance and significance today. They are not confined to Pakistan either, or even to Islam. They give rise to timeless universal questions relating to every religion: matters of peace and war, order and chaos, and the defence and suppression of fundamental human rights.

In view of the importance of this subject, there has been a growing demand to make *Mazhab ke Nam per Khoon* available to a much wider readership than those using the Urdu, Bengali and Indonesian languages.

For some years, Syed Barakat Ahmad was pressing me for permission to translate my book. Syed Barakat Ahmad had a doctorate in Arab history (from the American University of Beirut) and literature (from the University of Tehran). He served in the Indian diplomatic service and retired as India's High Commissioner to the West Indies. He was also an adviser to the Indian delegation to the United Nations, a fellow of the Indian Council of Historical Research and a student of Arabic teaching at the Al Azhar and Aligarh Universities.

Syed Barakat Ahmad suggested that as the original work in Urdu was addressed to readers who were familiar with Islamic terminology and the important events of early Islamic history, having been brought up in the Muslim cultural background, some changes would be necessary to make the translation of it into English fully comprehensible to readers less familiar with Islam. In view of this some portions were appropriately amended and, at his suggestion, explanations were provided wherever necessary.

Four years or so ago, when Syed Barakat Ahmad undertook this work, he was already suffering from an advanced stage of cancer of the bladder. Doctors had given him six months to live at the longest. He repeatedly wrote to me asking for prayers and expressing his desire that Allah might grant him the opportunity to finish not only the present work but many other projects he was undertaking at the same time.

It is sad indeed that the translator is no longer with us today, having died in early 1988. But, at the same time, one cannot but feel a deep sense of satisfaction at the thought that he was given an extended lease of life and did not die before he had completed most of the important works he had undertaken. During his few final years, one of his important works - which has drawn wide acclaim - is his book *Introduction to Quaranic Script*.

Just a few months before his demise, he was also able to write a very scholarly article, 'Muhammad and the Jews', which was acknowledged as a model of historical research. He was in extreme pain and discomfort during his last days, but he was an outstandingly brave man and continued to work almost till his last breath. May Allah rest his soul in eternal peace.

When the translation was sent to the publishers, they conveyed to me the opinion of one of the reviewers that the manuscript should be expanded to include an appraisal of the use of capital punishment for apostasy. They said that the text needed to be updated with reference to growing terrorist tendencies and militancy in some Muslim countries. In particular, what is understood of Khomeinism and Qaddafism by the West gives people a very negative impression of the peaceful intent and teachings of Islam. In view of this, it was felt that it would be highly appropriate if one or two chapters were added in order to discuss the subject in relation to the more widely known current events. Accordingly, two new chapters have been added; these were written in English and do not, of course, appear in the orginal Urdu text.

Finally, I would like to acknowledge my thanks to a number of people who have assisted in preparing the present version: Mansoor Ahmed Shah for transcribing from my notes and dictation; Malik Saifur Rehman, Abdul Momin Tahir and Munir Ahmed Javed, who collectively helped in finding references to the *hadith*; B. A. Rafiq for co-ordinating with the publishers; and the publishers' copy editor for rectifying typograhical errors.

Mirza Tahir Ahmad
Khalifatul Masih IV,
London 20 February 1989

CHAPTER 1

RELIGION DRIPS WITH BLOOD

Did our history begin with the curse of Cain? It is a gory tale of murder, assassination and torture in any event. So much blood has been spilled throughout history that the whole world could be painted red with it - with plenty to spare. When will man stop killing his fellow men? When will his thirst for blood ever be quenched?

Abel was the first man to be killed, by his brother, for no reason. The story of that murder has been preserved by the Quran and the Bible as a lesson to us all - it will remain as an example till the end of time. Study history, and one thing becomes clear: that man is an aggressive creature. His aggressiveness has been untamed by the growth of civilisation. Man is as cruel today as he was thousands of years ago. The story of his ruthlessness, his tyranny and his aggression is long and painful. The fire of human aggression has not been quenched even after thousands of years of savagery.

Assassination of individuals and the annihilation of whole groups of peoples are a repetitive theme of history. States have attacked states; countries have fought against their neighbours and against nations far from their borders. Hordes of people living in the steppes and deserts conquered nations with ancient civilisations; blood was shed by Caesar and by Alexander; Baghdad was destroyed by Hulagu and Gengiz; the soil of Kurukshetra ran red with the blood of Kauravas and Pandavas.

Sometimes blood was spilled in the name of honour, sometimes in the name of revenge for supposed wrongs. Sometimes angry hordes overran peaceful lands in search of food, sometimes in search of world domination. But more often the blood of man - created in God's image - was shed in the name of his Creator. Religion was used as an excuse for mass murder. Seeing this aspect of human nature makes one wonder if mankind is not the basest and most ruthless species on earth. One expects religion to teach man to be civilised, yet religion itself drips with blood. This fact recalls the incident which took place at the time of the creation of Adam[as], described by both the Quran and the Bible. The Quran says:

> And when thy Lord said to the angels, 'I am about to place a vicegerent in the earth,' they said, 'Wilt Thou place therein such as will cause disorder in it and shed blood? - and we glorify Thee with Thy praise and extol Thy holiness.' He answered, 'I know what you know not'. (2.35)

This dialogue between the angels and God is baffling because any book on religious history would seem to prove that the angels were right. If so, why did God refuse to accept their 'advice' or uphold their objection to His plan? It was, in fact, an objection to prophecy itself and ultimately to the prophethood of the Seal of Prophets, Muhammad[sa].

The history of religion in any part of the world at any time is the history of torture, repression, execution and crucifixion. It is disappointing indeed to find that religion, which is supposed to be the last refuge of peace in a world of war and conflict, is a cause of destruction and bloodshed. Religion itself is *not* the real cause of mass murder, however, and it is a mistake to think it is. Religion was not given to man to encourage killing.

When one discovers, with mixed feelings of satisfaction and surprise, that God did not make religion for this purpose, one receives a ray of hope. The vicegerent of God, whose creation the angels questioned, was really a great reformer. The religion he preached was named Islam - the religion of peace. The question remains: why, at first glance, does history create the impression that religion sanctions bloodshed and murder in the name of peace? The Quran points out very clearly why a cursory glance at history can lead one to such a conclusion. It cites the past to show that those who perpetuate brutality in religion's name are either anti-religious or people whose religion has been corrupted. There are also religious leaders who have no warmth, compassion, mercy or piety. To be honest, they are hypocrites with a lust for power - cruelty is their ruling passion. It would be a great mistake to associate religion with the misdeeds of such men. The real truth is that God - the Fountainhead of Mercy - does not allow the followers of any religion to oppress His people.

The Quran quotes many historical examples to prove this point. The early part of the prophets' lives is given by the Quran as a standard for religious reform or for preaching. If physical force had been allowed by God, then surely it would have been permitted by the founders of religions. It is quite clear that force is forbidden. Those followers who came long after the prophets and preached by force either inherited a religion corrupted by time or were themselves corrupt. They used force in the name of religion, yet their religion opposed the use of force.

The Quran's religious history is full of examples of force and violence used in the name of religion by people who had no religion. People were tortured in the name of Allah by those who had not the faintest clue about God. Noah[as], who called people to righteousness and piety, was not an oppressor - those who wished to suppress his voice were in the wrong. On hearing Noah's[as] message they said: 'If you don't desist, O Noah, you shall surely be one of those who are stoned.' (26.117)

The history of religious persecution, as told by the Quran, clearly shows that followers of true religion are the victims of violence. The Quran gives the example of Abraham[as], who called the people to God by using love, sympathy and humility. He had no sword . . . not a single weapon. But the elders of his people did exactly what the anti-religious opponents of Noah[as] had done. Abraham's[as] father, Azar, said: 'If you do not desist from your belief I shall stone you.' The words used by Azar were virtually identical to those used by Noah's[as] enemies. Both Noah[as] and Abraham[as] were insulted and humiliated, both were beaten and tortured, yet both accepted it all with patience and fortitude. Having lit the fire of oppression and mischief, the tormentors of Abraham[as] tried to burn him alive.

Those who opposed Lot[as] knew nothing whatsoever about religion. Yet they were his enemies and opposed him and his followers in religion's name. They threatened him with violence; they warned him that he and his followers would be banished. They did their best to stop him teaching his religion.

The persecutors of Shuaib[as] did the same and told him: 'Assuredly we will drive you out and the believers with you from our town and you shall have to return to our religion.' (7.89)

By citing these examples, the Quran proves there is a pattern of conversion to true religion and also to the force used by the enemies of truth against such conversion. Shuaib's[as] reply to the threats typifies the attitude of all God's prophets. He said: 'Even though we be unwilling?' Is it possible to change hearts by force, can a man be reconverted to a religion he has discarded after discovering it to be false? And can he be reconverted after he has discovered the truth of a new religion?

No dictator has ever been able to escape this logic. The historical fact is that the sword has never ruled and will never rule men's hearts. If the human body can be subdued by force, then the soul cannot. Belief is a thing of the heart. It is human nature which never changes. Innocent people who are sentenced to death in the name of religion by those who do not understand it will continue to raise their voice against this injustice. They will forever pose the question: 'Do you want us to stick to the beliefs our intelligence has rejected?' Whenever this question has been asked, enemies of religion across the world have accused the prophets of apostasy and sentenced them to death. Inhuman torture and punishments were invented . . . the story of violence is one which never ends.

Moses[as] and his followers met the same fate at the hands of the so-called religious heads of the time - Pharaoh, Haman and Korah - who said: 'Slay the sons of those who have believed with him and let their women live.' Conversion from one religion to another was not punished by the prophets, yet they and their followers were punished for the so-called apostasy. After Moses[as], Jesus[as] endured similar torture and violence which culminated in an attempt to kill him on the Cross. Bloodshed and violence have always been carried out in religion's name: their victims have throughout time been those found guilty of apostasy. Yet not a single revealed book sanctions the punishment of those who changed from one religion to another. If the texts of revealed Books have been altered by dishonest people, one can hardly blame the Books themselves. By their very nature, Books revealed to God's prophets cannot teach violence.

Making reference to the history of religions, the Quran proves that the prophets and their followers were victims of violence; victims who, nonetheless, accepted brutality with patience. It is beyond one's belief that people who change faiths can be tortured in the name of religion, and prophets of God, who are sent to convert us, cannot accept it either. It makes nonsense of their own mission. The Quran also tells how a prophet's followers are punished for conversion not only during his life, but for hundreds of years after his death. Such oppression has no sanction from God.

Then there is the Quranic story of the people of the cave. These Christians were persecuted for 300 years, and I have seen the places where these poor people were tortured - the amphitheatres intended for gladiatorial combat with bulls and lions. It was in these places that naked Christians were thrown to hungry wild animals. The animals howled and made short shrift of the defenceless Christians. Sometimes these 'apostates' were thrown to bulls which had been starved for several days. The starving creatures bellowed and snorted and, with hissing screeches, attacked. The Christians were gored or trampled to death. And after this festival of blood, the laughing Romans returned joyfully home. The 'apostates' had been fittingly punished. But while the Christians' legs trembled, their hearts beat strongly with faith in God.

Their persecution went on intermittently for three centuries. And when they found no place to hide, they fled underground to the catacombs. These long labyrinths exist today and they remind us that the Christians could live with insects, scorpions and snakes but not with religious leaders in their fine clothes.

As well as those people who fled underground - *Ashabi Kah* Quran also mentions other Christians who believed in the Unity of and were burned alive for their pains. God says:

> By the heaven having mansions of stars, and the Promised Day, and witness and he to whom witness is borne, cursed be the Fellows of Trench - the fire fed with fuel - when they sat by it and they were witnesses of what they did to the believers. And they hated them not l *only* because they believed in Allah, the Almighty, the Praiseworthy, to Whom belongs the Kingdom of the heavens and the earth; and Allah is Witness over all things. (85.2-10)

The enormity of these atrocities is made worse because of the so-called religious protectors who actually *prevent* worship of Allah; their victims feel a greater anguish from being prevented from worshipping than they do from torture itself. The Quran says: 'And who is more unjust than the man who prohibits the name of Allah being glorified in Allah's mosques and seeks to destroy them?' (2.115) So the Quran totally rejects the use of force to suppress religious freedom. It declares that though such suppression takes place, true believers never use force to preach the name of Allah.

So far we have told the story of the persecution of prophets who came before the time when God's light was to illuminate the world. But eventually the sun of eternal truth rose on the skies of the Arab peninsula and the world was soon to bask in the light of Muhammad's[sa] message.

For thousands of years the world had awaited the greatest prophet. One hundred and twenty-four thousand prophets had lived and died in the hope of welcoming this Seal of the Prophets. The man for whom the whole world was created finally appeared, reflecting the full glory of his Creator. He was greater than all the prophets; his religion was complete. But he, too, was persecuted and his persecution was without precedence. Our Master and Lord, Prophet Muhammad[sa], endured every conceivable form of punishment, torture and torment suffered by the earlier prophets and their followers.

Early Muslims were laid out in the blazing sun. Burning stones were put on their chests; they were dragged through the streets of Mecca like dead animals. They were shunned, and kept hungry and thirsty. They were thrown into dungeons, their belongings were seized and their families were broken up. Pregnant women were thrown off camels, their inevitable deaths the cause of merriment. Their dead bodies were cut asunder - the liver of the Prophet's[sa] uncle was even eaten. They were cut down with swords and pierced by arrows. The Prophet[sa] was stoned by ffians and vagabonds and was chased and pelted by urchins till the bblestones of Taif ran red with his blood. And at the battle-ground of ıud the Prophet[sa] was seriously wounded.

This bloodshed took place in the name of religion, because Muslims id Rabbunallaha, our Lord, is Allah. This persecution and torture was rpetrated in the name of religion because, according to the polytheists Mecca, the Prophet[sa] and the Muslims were apostates. The polytheist called the Prophet[sa] and his followers *'Sabi'* - people who discard their ancestral religion and adopt a new one. In order to put down this 'evil', the Meccans adopted methods of torture and suppression which had been used by their predecessors. Muhammad[sa] and his followers suffered patiently and with fortitude for a long time to prove that evil is caused by anti-religious people and not by followers of the truth.

The Prophet[sa], exalted by Allah to a position with no equal, showed his persecutors only unsurpassable love, mercy and forgiveness in return for their evil. When victory finally came and the polytheists of Mecca were subdued by the Prophet[sa], he ordered a general amnesty. There was no massacre and no punishment for his persecutors. No arrests were made. No executions took place. Instead of retribution there was the Quranic proclamation: 'Let no reproach be on you this day. May Allah forgive you. He is the most merciful of the merciful.'

That day the cruellest of the cruel were pardoned. Those who had tormented helpless slaves on the burning sand were forgiven. Those who had dragged Muslims through the streets like dead animals were absolved. Those who had breached the peace were pardoned, as were those who had stoned defenceless Muslims - even the woman who had eaten the liver of the Prophet's[sa] uncle.

If the history of the world from Adam[as] to the present day were ever lost - and with it the record of every persecution and of every charter of human rights - a glance at the life of the Prophet[sa] would more than prove that true religion does not cause hatred, persecution, repression or the suppression of thought.

But the Prophet[sa] did not confine his teachings to calling for religious tolerance. Since the Prophet of Islam[sa] is 'A mercy for the universe' (21.108), a general proclamation is made by the Quran: 'There shall be no compulsion in religion.' Compulsion is unnecessary because, 'Guidance and error have been clearly distinguished' (2.257) and there is no possibility of confusing the two. On the face of it, this proclamation seems unusual and anomalous. On one hand there was an arbitrary authority, hell-bent on wiping out a small group of people becuase of their 'apostasy' with every means at its disposal. And when this group of 'apostasy' gained power, it was told by the Quran to proclaim that:

There shall be no compulsion in religion, for guidance and error have been clearly distinguished; so whoever refuses to be led by those who transgress and believes in Allah, has surely grasped a strong handle - one which knows no breaking. (2.257)

But it must be noted that this proclamation is made in the second chapter of the Quran, *Al-Baqarah*, which was revealed in the first two or three years after the Prophet's[sa] arrival in Medina, a place where Muslims were not only free from Meccan persecution but also held power. What could be a more human and generous proclamation of peace from a prophet who, only a year or two earlier, had been persecuted for 'changing his religion'?

People who persecute in the name of religion are totally ignorant of the essence of religion. Religion is a metamorphosis of hearts. Religion is not politics and its adherents do not make up political parties. Neither is it a nationality with limited loyalties, nor a country with geographical borders. It is the transformation of hearts - transformation for the good of the soul. The home of religion is in the depths of the heart. It is beyond the sway of the sword. Mountains are not moved by the sword, nor are hearts changed by force. While persecution in the name of religion is the repetitive theme in the history of human aggression, freedom of conscience is the Quran's repetitive theme.

The Prophet[sa] was asked again and again to proclaim: 'This is the truth from your Lord; let him who will, believe, and let him who will, disbelieve.' (18.30) Truth is obviously a matter of the heart; it has nothing to do with force. Once it has been seen it cannot be blotted out by any power. Hence the Quran's assertion that once truth is known it is our choice to accept or reject it. Yet, elsewhere, the Quran says: 'Verily, this is a reminder: so whosoever wishes may take to the way that leads to his Lord.' (76.30) No charter of human rights can surpass the clarity of the Quranic phrase *faman Shaa'* (whosoever wishes). The word 'whosoever' is all inclusive. It is surprising that after such a clear declaration anyone could possibly think that Islam supports the use of force.

Again, in the 39th chapter of the Quran, the Prophet[sa] is ordered to tell unbelievers: 'It is Allah I worship in sincerest obedience.' Now, as far as you are concerned, 'Worship what you like besides Him.' (39.16)

Since freedom of conscience - freedom to believe and to preach - is the cornerstone of religion, and repression of religious heresy is the aim of anti-religious forces, the Quran lays great emphasis on the freedom of conversion. The last line of Chapter 109 of the Quran sums up the basic principle of a true religion. 'For you, your religion and for me, my religion.' In an earlier passage (10.108), God refers to the same principle by asking a rhetorical question. Addressing the Holy Prophet[sa], He says: 'If thy Lord had enforced His will, surely all those on earth would have believed, without exception? Will thou, then, take it upon thyself to force people to become believers?' In the scheme of creation, man must have complete free will to believe or otherwise; there is no compulsion; a man must use his reason and understanding. After all, faith is a gift given by God to those He thinks deserve it.

One hundred and twenty-four thousand prophets were sent by God and showed, by their teaching and example, that the bearers of the divine message are the oppressed, not the oppressors. The prophets won over hearts by moral and spiritual strength, not by physical force. It is a great tragedy that the ordained priests and the turbaned Mullahs with their flowing robes of 'piety' became the tormentors of the innocent in the name of oppressed prophets. They monopolised religion, yet they knew nothing of it. They claimed to protect the honour of their prophets by maligning others, by spreading malicious lies and, above all, by perpetrating crimes of violence which shamed humanity. They did it before the birth of the Holy Prophet[sa]. They do it still.

In medieval Europe, the so-called followers of Christ[as] - the popes and the prelates, cardinals and canons, and the elders of the Church - wrote a chapter of terror into the history books. St Augustine called it 'righteous persecution which the Church of Christ inflicts upon the impious'.[1] Today's Christian historians admit that this 'righteous persecution', inflicted in Christ's[as] name, was a disgrace to the Church.

Madame Tussaud's waxworks museum in London has a strange, moving and terrifying exhibition of this persecution. The museum was originally founded in Paris in 1770 and moved to England in 1802. Its walls are lined with waxworks of famous and infamous people. Its Chamber of Horrors is a kind of underground dungeon. The figures there have been modelled into such uncanny likenesses that you can almost see them breathing. Many visitors there have stopped to ask directions from a friendly looking curator, only to find they have been talking to a dummy! On display are the death-masks from the guillotined heads of Louis XVI and Marie Antoinette, which were personally cast by Madame Tussaud. There is an authentic gallows with other instruments of torture: pillory, stocks, whipping-post, ducking-stool, iron maiden rack, galleys, bed of Procrustes, cross, gibbet, halter and many others. Some exhibits are so gruesome that they are covered with screens to keep them away from children and squeamish adults.

It is a strange world where a man can rise to the heights of pro-phethood and talk with his Creator, then sink to the depths of becoming a priest and questioning Joan of Arc about her visions of angels. He can sink even lower and become an inquisitor. The instruments of torture shown at Madame Tussaud's tell the tragic story of the Spanish and French Inquisitions. Innocent people were tortured for their so-called apostasy; they were forced to confess that they had recanted from the true religion. When they refused, they were whipped and flogged, put on the rack, lynched, impaled, pilloried, branded and burned. The victims either confessed or died a miserable death. These dignitaries of the Church in all their finery, who tortured innocent Christians, remind one of Christ[sa] with his crown of thorns, bleeding on the Cross and crying with a loud voice: 'Eli, Eli, lama sabachthani?' (Matthew 27:46). These were the people who symbolically consumed the flesh and blood of Christ[as] at Communion services, yet could not recall that the Pharisees had asked Pontius Pilate to crucify Christ[as] because he had 'apostasised' and abandoned the religion of his forefathers. But the crucifixion of Christ[as] pales into insignificance when compared with the Inquisition of medie-val Christians. It is with a sense of relief and, indeed, pride that Islam, with its declaration of 'no compulsion in the matter of belief', has finally closed the door on such atrocities in religion's name. But this sense of relief and pride is only short-lived. Any Muslim will lower his head with shame when he sees today's *ulema* vying with what the Christian priests of medieval Europe did to devise new ways of suppressing freedom of thought and conscience. And yet these are the very *ulema* who claim to protect the honour of the Holy Prophet[sa] whom the Quran describes as a 'mercy for the universe'.

These *ulema* claim to be the very personification of mercy, but their hearts are without compassion. Instead, they are filled with anger. The use of force in the name of religion has now become part of their faith. In the name of God's holy water - sent to cool our tempers - they kindle the fires of hatred and anger in the hearts of the innocent. The followers of the Prince of Peace[sa], whose blood cleansed barbaric Arabia, are now being persuaded to murder helpless people. In the name of the protector of poor people's unguarded homes his followers are encouraged to rob the homes of people who are powerless to defend themselves. In the name of the Prophet[sa] who protected the honour of even ruffians' wives, the happy and loving marriages of Muslim women are anulled and transformed into adulterous relationships. In the name of the builder of the first mosque in Medina, who offered it to the Christians of Najran for Sunday services, in the name of the Prophet[sa] who taught his followers to respect the temples of other faiths, today's *ulema* incite the masses to destroy the mosques of a small group of people whose lives are devoted to the spreading of *shahada*.[2] The unjust acts the Prophet[sa] condemned and banned forever are now being perpetrated in his very name. What would the Holy Prophet[sa] think if he could see the *ulema* of his *umma* falsely accusing the elders of other Muslim groups of all sorts of misdeeds and shouting abuse about women and housewives? How will an agnostic react to this demonstration of 'religious zeal'? What Muslim could think, even for a moment, that our Prophet[sa], would have advised the *ulema* of his *umma* to deliver provocative, disruptive speeches; or that he would have ordered them to deliver such fiery sermons that entire villages of poor and helpless people were set ablaze? Not satisfied with all this, could the Prince of Peace[sa] have told religious leaders to treat as apostates all those Muslims whose understanding of Islam did not conform to their own? Would he have sanctioned the killing of them and their women and the destruction of their mosques - said to be the only divine way to blot out apostasy?

These are the questions we should all think seriously about. Muslims should consider the attitude of these *ulema*. For suppression, torture, execution, arson and the razing of mosques are not the Prophet's[sa] tradition. Every stone in the streets of Mecca over which the so-called apostates were dragged bears witness to this. Every grain of burning

Arabian sand where helpless people were tortured for accepting Islam does the same. The cobbles of Taif, where the blood of the Holy Prophet[sa] was spilled, bear witness to the fact that our great Master - mercifully - did not teach that religious belief was compulsory, that he did not order the burning of houses of worship in the name of worship or the dishonouring of women in the name of honour. Muslims hang their heads in shame and their souls cry out over today's religious leaders who preach violence in the name of the Prophet[sa].

CHAPTER 2

THE PREACHING OF ISLAM: TWO CONFLICTING VIEWS

1 When every method of persuasion (over 13 years of preaching) had failed, the Prophet[sa] took to the sword . . . that sword removed evil and mischief, the impurities of the heart and the filth of the soul. The sword did something more. It removed their blindness - they could see the light of truth - and it also cured them of their arrogance; arrogance which prevents people from accepting the truth . . . stiff necks and proud heads bowed with humility.

Maulana Abul Ala Maududi

Muhammad preached Islam with a sword in one hand and the Quran in the other.

Prof. Wilfred Cantwell Smith

2 The critics are blind. They cannot see that the only sword Muhammad wielded was the sword of mercy, compassion, friendship and forgiveness - the sword that conquers enemies and purifies hearts. His sword was sharper than the sword of steel.

Gyanandra Dev Sharma Shastri

These are two conflicting views about the way in which the message of Islam was conveyed to the world. Critics, especially orientalists, claim that the wars the Prophet of Islam[sa] fought were offensive wars and that people were converted by force. According to objective historians, however, this view is not upheld by the facts. The Prophet[sa] did not use force to preach and all the battles he fought were defensive. The expansion of Islam was due to the Prophet's[sa] spiritual and moral power.

Nevertheless, the view that Islam was spread by force is, unfortunately, held by some Muslim leaders. They, like the orientalists, divide the life of the Prophet[sa] into Meccan and Medinite periods. They maintain that at Mecca he was weak and powerless, hence that compromising and submissive attitude of peaceful co-existence. Then, having gained some power at Medina, he resorted to the sword, according to this school of thought.

Had he not done so there would have been no spiritual revolution in Arabia and Islam would not have spread. The late Maulana Abul Ala Maududi[1] was a leading proponent of this view. In his book. *Al-Jihad fil Islam*, the Maulana says:

> The Messenger of Allah[sa] invited the Arabs to accept Islam for 13 years. He used every possible means of persuasion, gave them incontrovertible arguments and proofs, showed them miracles and put before them his life as an example of piety and morality. In short, he used every possible means of communication, but his people refused to accept Islam.

It grieves my heart to quote the rest of this passage but it needs to be set out.

> When every method of persuasion had failed, the Prophet[sa] took to the sword.
>
> That sword removed evil mischief, the impurities of evil and the filth of the soul. The sword did something more - it removed their blindness so that they could see the light of truth, and also cured them of their arrogance; arrogance which prevents people from accepting the truth, stiff necks and proud heads bowed with humility.
>
> As in Arabia and other countries, Islam's expansion was so fast that within a century a quarter of the world accepted it. This conversion took place because the sword of Islam tore away the veils which had covered men's hearts.[2]

The above statement is doubly unfortunate because it was made by a Muslim scholar who claimed to be *mizaj-shanasi-Rasul*, the one who found himself in complete harmony with the mind and heart of the Prophet[sa], so much so that he acquires a measure of authority in explaining the true meanings of the words and deeds of the Prophet[sa] - a claim which, if accepted, would give the claimant as much or more right to represent than the Holy Prophet[sa] enjoyed *vis-à-vis* his understanding of the Word of God. This means that the Maulana's understanding is tragic beyond words - it has been made by a Muslim leader and repeats a baseless assertion of Islam's enemies. It is the biased orientalists who accused the Prophet[sa] of converting people by force. The Maulana's phraseology appears to glorify Islam, but in reality it endorses the accusation of the European critics of Islam. R. Dozy said: 'Muhammad's generals preached Islam with a sword in one hand and the Quran in the other.' Smith asserted that it was not the generals but the Prophet[sa] himself who 'preached with a sword in one hand and the Quran in the other'. George Sale wrote: 'When the followers of the Prophet increased in number he claimed that God had allowed him to attack the unbelievers so that idolatry be destroyed and true religion be established.'

The Revd Dr C. G. Pfander, who was actively engaged in missionary work among Indian Muslims during the latter part of the nineteenth century, provoked great unrest by writing controversial tracts to expose, as he put it, 'The false Prophet of Islam'. In one such tract he said:

1. For 13 years Muhammad preached his new religion in conciliatory terms and with great patience.

2. Now (in Medina) he became *Al-Nabiyyussaif*, 'The sword-wielding Prophet', and since then Islam's strongest argument has been the sword.

3. If we study the behaviour of Muhammad's[sa] followers we notice that they thought it was not necessary for them to follow a religious and moral code. God demanded from them only one thing: that they should fight for God with swords, arrows, daggers and sabres to continue to kill.[3]

And after this introduction the Revd Dr Pfander concluded: 'You have to choose between Jesus, Word of God, and Hazrat Muhammad, son of Abdullah; between one who devoted his life to acts of piety and one who dedicated his life to the sword.'[4]

Aloy Spranger, Henry Copey and many other critics of Islam followed the same line of attack on both Islam and the Prophet[sa]. Washington Irving went a step further; printed on the title page of one of his books is an imaginary painting of the Prophet[sa] with a sword in one hand and the Quran in the other.[5]

If one compares all that has been quoted above with the opening quotation of Maulana Maududi's *Al-Jihad fil Islam*, one finds the Prophet's[sa] critics in agreement. Both the Maulana and the orientalists maintained that Islam had a violent nature. Yet, despite this belief, the Maulana believed in Islam while they rejected it. Apart from the wording, there is no difference between paragraphs 1, 2 and 3 of the quotation from Maulana Maududi above and the quotation from Dr Pfander above. But one shows the respect of a Muslim; the other, the sarcasm of a bitter critic.

The snide remarks of the orientalists about the Prophet of Islam[sa] are as unsurprising as they are hurtful. They are sometimes made out of ignorance, but mostly out of malice. The hostility towards Islam colours the objectivity of even the most balanced historian. But most hurtful of all are the writings of Muslims who claim devoutly to follow the

Prophet[sa], yeι present him, either through ignorance or arrogance, as a barbarian who wielded the sword to convert and conquer.

Maulana Maududi was not convinced of the inherent beauty of Islam or that it could conquer hearts by its spiritual force alone, either in the past or present. He said:

> Human relations and associations are so integrated that no state can have complete freedom of action within its own principles, unless those same principles are in force in a neighbouring country. Therefore, Muslim groups will not be content with the establishment of an Islamic state in one area alone. Depending on their resources, they should try to expand in all directions. On one hand, they will spread their ideology and on the other they will invite people of all nations to accept their creed, for salvation lies only in it. *If their Islamic state has power and resources it will fight and destroy non-Islamic governments and establish Islamic states in their place.*[6]

Maulana Maududi supports Sir William Muir's twisted views of the Prophet[sa] and of Islam. In his biography of the Prophet[sa], which he wrote to expose 'the false Prophet of Islam'[7] at the request of Dr Pfander, Sir William Muir said: 'The sword of Mahomet, and the Coran are the most fatal enemies of civilisation, liberty and truth which the world has yet known.'[8]

The great Hindu leader, Gandhiji, in his earlier days, must have been influenced by a distorted picture of Islam such as this when he said: 'Islam was born in an atmosphere of violence. At that time its determining force was the sword and even today it is the sword.' But Gandhiji was an observer of great insight and subsequently he corrected himself and wrote in *Young India*: 'The more I study the more I discover that the strength of Islam does not lie in the sword.'

Other Hindus - even Arya Samajists, who made an objective study of Islam - followed Gandhiji in his 'discovery'. Pandit Gyanandra Dev Sharma Shastri said:

> Biased critics of Islam and especially those who want to provoke Hindu - Muslim riots in the country say that Hazrat Muhammad after acquiring power in Medina could not maintain his facade of mercy and kindness. There he used force and violence and became a murderous prophet to achieve his life-long aim of power, status and wealth. He fell short of his own ideal of patience, moderation and endurance. But this is the view of those observers who are prejudicial and partisan, who are narrow-minded and whose eyes are covered by a veil of ignorance. They see fire instead of light, ugliness instead of beauty and evil instead of good. They

distort and present every good quality as a great vice. It reflects their own depravity. . . .

The critics are blind. They cannot see that the only 'sword' Muhammad wielded was the sword of mercy, compassion, friendship and forgiveness - the sword that conquers enemies and purifies their hearts. His sword was sharper than the sword of steel.[9]

No comment! One only wishes that Maulana Maududi, a follower of the Prophet Muhammad[sa], had been as fair to the Prophet[sa] as a follower of Krishna[as] had been. Non-Muslims who have studied the history of Islam have had to admit that the Prophet[sa] was not only magnanimous and kind, but also a paragon of human virtues. Another Hindu, the editor of the *Sat Updaish*, wrote:

Some people say that Islam was preached by the sword, but we cannot agree with this view. What is forced on people is soon rejected. Had Islam been imposed on people through oppression, there would have been no Islam today. Why? Because the Prophet of Islam had spiritual power, he loved humanity and he was guided by the ideal of ultimate good.[10]

The anti-Muslim stance of the Arya Samaj movement is well known. Its founder, Swami Dayanand, was highly critical of Islam and its Prophet[sa] and yet the following statement was made by a Hindu at a meeting sponsored by the Arya Samaj in Lahore. The editor of the *Vedic Magazine* and a former professor of Gurukul, Kangri Ram Dev, said:

Sitting in Medina, Muhammad Sahib (peace be to him) held the Arabs spellbound; he filled them with spiritual strength; strength that makes *devtas* [gods] out of men . . . it is incorrect to say that Islam spread with the force of the sword. It is a fact that the sword was never wielded to propagate Islam. If religion can be spread by force then let anyone try it today.[11]

The last sentence of the above passage is a challenge no one would ever accept - not even Maulana Maududi. No sword can change a heart and turn belief into disbelief. There was a long chain of prophets before the Prophet of Islam[sa] and it is an historical truth that every prophet was opposed by force. Every time a prophet taught the true religion he was opposed by the sword and yet true religion spread and the sword failed to cut it back. If all past prophets and their followers could stand against the sword's might, how is it possible that Muhammad[sa] could have adopted a different approach and taken to the sword - the instrument of oppression, not truth? There is no greater injustice than to accuse him of using force to change people's beliefs.

Another non-Muslim scholar, Dr D. W. Leitz, in rebutting this false charge, based his argument on the Quran itself. He said:

> All these arguments, advanced to prove that the purpose of *jihad* was to spread Islam by force, are contradicted by the Quran. The Quran says that the purpose of *jihad* is to protect mosques, churches, synagogues and cloisters.[12]

After such a clear defence of the Prophet[sa], let so-called Muslims who accuse him of wielding the sword answer this Quranic question: 'Do they not ponder over the Quran, or is it that their hearts are locked up from within? (47.25) Maulana Maududi, the author of the voluminous commentary on the Quran, *Tafhim-ul-Quran*, must have read this verse many times. Did it not occur to him that interpreting the Quran for political purposes might lead the commentator astray? The Maulana then says:

> This was the policy which was adopted by the Prophet[sa] and his rightly guided caliphs. Arabia, where the Muslim Party was first formed, was the first to be put down. After this, the Prophet[sa] sent invitations to all neighbouring countries, but did not wait to see whether these invitations were accepted. As soon as he acquired power, he started the conflict with the Roman Empire. Abu Bakr became the leader of the Party after the Prophet[sa] and attacked both the Roman and Persian Empires and Umar finally won the war.[13]

This is virtually a declaration of war against all non-Muslim neighbouring states - they are safe only as long as the Muslim state is weak. Had the above passage been written by a Marxist historian from the Communist Party, one would not have given it a second glance. But it is the considered opinion of a Muslim leader of Maulana Maududi's stature. As such, it is certainly far more insulting to the Prophet[sa] than all that Muir, Pfander, Smith and other critics of Islam have written. The above passage was translated from the Maulana's original Urdu. The words: 'Muslim Party' were used deliberately by Maududi. He was degrading the Muslim *umma* to the status of a political party. He was well aware of the difference between the two words, for in another book he said: 'The other word the Quran has used for "party" is *umma*.'[14] Having dubbed Muslims a politcal party, the Maulana either subconsciously or, more likely, deliberately, equates the Prophet[sa] with a political party leader, assigning to him the morals of a politician. How else can one explain the following passage written by the Maulana?

> After this the Prophet[sa] sent invitations to all the neighbouring countries, but he did not wait to see whether these invitations were accepted or not. As soon as he acquired more power he started the conflict with the Roman Empire.

It is amazing that a Muslim scholar could even by implication suggest that the Prophet was guilty of a Hitler-style invasion - *Naaudhu billah*.[15] The Prophet[sa] was the Prince of Peace, not an invader. Maulana Maududi loved political power and, unfortunately, this colours his interpretation of Islamic history. But Islam does not need politics to prop it up. In Bengal, now Bangladesh, Muslims were an infinitesimal minority in the middle of the eighteenth century when the British took over the administration from the Mughals. By the time Bengal became independent in 1947 it had a Muslim majority. Muslims had no political control of the area nor was there any migration of Muslims from northern India during British rule. This increase in Bengal's Muslim population was owing to peaceful conversion by travelling *sufis*, the roving Muslim missionaries and the Imams of the village mosques.

Thomas Arnold's observation on the subject is significant. He said: 'Islam has gained its greatest and most lasting missionary triumphs in times and places in which its political power has been weakest.'[16] Maulana Maududi probably never read the history of Islam in Bengal, Malaysia or Indonesia. He was so enthralled by the Turko-Afghan and Mughal conquests that he never had time to note that the largest Muslim country in the world, Indonesia, never had a Muslim conquerer - that there was no fighting nor any violence there. That was the case also in Malaysia.

The Prophet[sa] was obviously innocent. He took up the sword only in self-defence and only when oppression became unbearable. Here is what an objective Sikh has to say on the subject:

> In the beginning the Prophet's enemies made life difficult for him and his followers. So the Prophet asked his followers to leave their homes and migrate to Medina. He preferred migration to fighting his own people, but when oppression went beyond the pale of tolerance he took up his sword in self-defence. Those who believe religion can be spread by force are fools who neither know the ways of religion nor the ways of the world. They are proud of this belief because they are a long, long way away from the Truth.[17]

Who knows better: a Sikh journalist or the *mizaj shanasi nubuwwat*?[18]

18

CHAPTER 3

A REBUTTAL OF MAUDUDIAN PHILOSOPHY

The Hindu rivivalist movements took an aggressive turn in the early 1920s after the failure of the joint Hindu - Muslim *khilafat* movement. The Hindu Mahasabha, founded at Hardwar in 1914 by Pandit Madan Mohan Malaviya (1861-1946), joined the Arya Samaj in its campaign of *shuddi* (reconversion and purification of Muslims, initially in the Punjab, the United Provinces (now Uttar Pradesh), the Deccan and other parts of India. By forcing Muslims to 'wash away their pollution' with total immersion in a river or water-tank, Hindu gangs provoked communal rioting. Between 1922 and 1926 over 200 Hindu - Muslim clashes were reported. Verbal and written attacks on Islam and Islam's Prophet[sa] became widespread. In their religious zeal, the writers of *shuddi* literature made scurrilous attacks on the Holy Prophet[sa]. An Arya Samaj preacher, Pandit Kalicharan Sharma, wrote his own account. He emphasised the Prophet's[sa] alleged immorality and the fact that he married to 'correct' the view of history. His book, *Vichitra Jiwan* (*Strange Life*), also stressed 'the spread of Islam by the sword'. All Muslims, according to Pandit Sharma, were intent on looting, arson and rape. In May 1924, a Lahore book-seller, Rajpal, published an Urdu tract by an anonymous author criticising the Holy Prophet[sa]. The tract, *Rangila Rasul* (*Playboy Prophet*) suggests that all great religious leaders are associated with sets of ideas and symbols. For instance, the founder of Arya Samaj, Swami Dayanand, had glorified celibacy and closely identified his reforms with the Vedas. Similarly, the life and faith of the Prophet of Islam[sa] were linked closely with relationships with women. Rajpal was later murdered by two Muslim youths, which led to Hindu - Muslim rioting. Another Hindu wrote an article, 'A trip to hell', in *Risala-i-Vartman* describing the Prophet[sa] in hell and elaborating on his sufferings and 'sins'.

The Ahmadis of undivided India immediately got themselves together and defeated the reconversion movement on its own ground. The Imam of the Ahmadiyyah Movement in Islam at the time, Mirza Bashiruddin Mahmud Ahmad, also took a positive step. He decided that there should be inter-faith conferences where the leaders of different faiths should meet and explain their beliefs in order to pull down the walls of ignorance and prejudice. He set up an annual conference for just this purpose. It was called *Yaum-i-Paishwayan-i-Madhabib* (The Day of Religious Founders). On that day, for instance, a Muslim would speak of the greatness of Krishna[as] or Buddha[as], while a Hindu would talk of Islam's Holy Prophet[sa], putting right misunderstandings about him which were being spread by propagandists. The Ahmadi attitude during this unfortunate time of calumny and hatred was that non-Muslims should be educated and given the message of love and peace which the Prophet of Islam[sa] gave the world. Accusations and sectarian diatribes do not help a missionary preach his faith. He should instead emphasise the good points of his religion. The Imam of the Ahmadiyyah Movement also persuaded the government of India - then British - to strengthen the law to protect the honour of religious leaders. The Punjab governor, William Hailey, who was briefed by Mirza Bashiruddin Mahmud Ahmad, recommended that the government of India change the law by banning material blatantly offensive to religious feeling.[1] The government accepted this recommendation. A bill was accordingly drafted to add a new section to the Indian Penal Code, 295A, which made it an offence to insult or to attempt to insult the religious beliefs of any class of people. The bill was passed in 1927 by the Legislative Assembly.

But Indian Muslims were very upset and indignant at this time. A Muslim calligrapher, Abdul Rashid, outraged by such malicious attacks on the Holy Prophet's[sa] life, murdered Swami Shraddhanand, a *shuddi* leader. Rashid was tried and hanged. Thousands of Delhi Muslims went to the Delhi District jail to collect his body and he was buried as a martyr. This glorification of murder enraged the Hindus, who called Islam a religion of violence and force which relied on *jihad* and not reason or virtue.[2] A young journalist, Abul Ala Maududi, answered these accusations in a series of articles in *Al-Jamiyat*, the newspaper of the Jamiyat Ulama-i-Hind. These articles were subsequently published in book form as *Al-Jihad fil Islam*.

In the first part of this book, Maududi convincingly proved that the wars fought by the Prophet of Islam[sa] were defensive. He fought to establish freedom of conscience and opposed all attempts to suppress the peaceful work of preaching Islam. Having convinced the reader that Islam did indeed establish the freedom of conscience, the Maulana himself seems to cast doubt on his own argument by adding this rider:

> That freedom of conscience is limited to faith and religion only. It does not mean that people have freedom to commit sin. Islam does not permit the use of force for conversion, but force may be used - in fact, *should* be used - to prevent people from doing wrong. Non-Muslim countries and cultures cannot be allowed to practice immoral deeds and force used to keep these countries free of vice should be clearly distinguished from that used to convert people to Islam.

Thus, the Maulana evolved a tortuous method of interpreting the Quran and the tradition (hadith) of the Prophet[sa] to prove his point.

Maulana Maududi goes a little deeper in discussing the use of force and explains the purpose of verse 29 of Chapter 9 in the Quran. Quoting it out of context, he says:

> The words: 'Until they pay the *jizya*' fully explain the purpose of war [prevention of vice]. If the words were: 'until they accept Islam' then, of course, one could say that Islam uses force to spread its faith. But the words, 'until they pay the *jizya*' are clear. Consent to pay the *jizya* ends the war. After this, the life and property of non-Muslims are inviolable, whether or not they accept Islam.

Maulana Maududi began writing his book to prove that Islam gives complete freedom of conscience and that the Holy Prophet[sa] went to war because his opponents were suppressing that very freedom. This was in answer to non-Muslim claims that Islam is based on two main principles: the forcing of people to do good and the prevention of them from indulging in vice. Since forcing people to do good is against the freedom of conscience, Islam refrains from it. But the Maulana is a little forgetful, for he quotes the Quranic words which say that a war should be stopped after non-Muslims have agreed to pay the *jizya*. How could a war, begun purely to prevent vice, ever be won if the enemy pays the *jizya* without promising to wipe out vice? The Maulana's aim was to impose the poll tax. Since an agreement had been reached for its payment, the second principle of Islam, prevention of vice, had been conveniently forgotten.

The final part of Maulana Maududi's logic, however, nullifies the very purpose for which he wrote this book. He says:

> When all methods of persuasion failed, the Prophet[sa] took to the sword. That sword removed mischief, the impurities of evil and the filth of the soul. The sword did something more - it removed their blindness so they could see the light of truth - and it also cured them of their arrogance:

21

arrogance which prevents people from accepting the truth, stiff necks and proud heads bowed with humility.

As in Arabia, so in other countries, Islam's expansion was so fast that within a century a quarter of the world accepted Islam. This conversion took place because the sword of Islam cut away the veils which had covered men's hearts.[3]

This portion of the Maulana's reasoning defeats his promise that Islam establishes freedom of conscience. It also is repugnant to the spirit of Islam. One mistake leads to another. Finally, after 137 pages of sophistry, the Maulana declares: 'While it is incorrect to say that Islam converts with the sword, it is also wrong to say that the sword did not play any role in conversion'.[4]

The Maulana began his book with the declared intention of proving that the wars fought by the Holy Prophet[sa] were 'defensive'. He fought to establish freedom of conscience, yet ends up joining hands with Islam's enemies. In doing so, the Maulana opens the doors for an orientalist onslaught. The prestige he enjoys among a small, but vocal, minority of Western-educated Muslims helps the orientalists, who bolster their anti-*jihad* arguments with the Maulana's brandished sword to 'play a role in the preaching of Islam'.

Less than two years after the Hijrah (the Prophet's[sa] migration from Mecca to Medina), his companions were confronted by a thousand Meccans, determined to blot out Islam, its Prophet[sa] and his followers. It was dawn on Friday, 17th March AD 623 (17 Ramadan, 2 AH) when the Meccans with 700 camels and a cavalry of 100 horses began descending towards the valley of Badr from the slope of Aqanqal, twenty miles south of Medina. There were just 313 Muslims there to defend Islam. They had only two horses and were so short of arms that when Ukkashah's sword was broken during the fighting, the Prophet[sa] could only replace it with a wooden club, which he used instead. Their situation became so desperate that the Prophet[sa] cried out: 'Allah! If this small band of Muslims is annihilated today, no one will be left to worship Thee!'

As Montgomery Watt puts it, Abu Jahl was 'presumably hoping to get rid of Muhammad once and for all'.[5] Will Durant agrees with Watt: 'If Mohammed had been defeated his career might have ended there and then.'[6] Abu Jahl's hopes were, however, not fulfilled and the Muslims successfully defended themselves against the well-equipped and far superior Meccan forces.

Islamic history has preserved the names of all 313 Companions of the

Prophet[sa] who defended Islam in the valley of Badr. One wonders what role the sword played in converting these 300-odd Muslims. Among them were Abu Bakr, Umar, Uthman and Ali, who succeeded the Prophet[sa] as his caliphs. Was it the sword which removed the 'dross' from their hearts? Then there were Awf b. Harith, Umar b. Salimah, Muawwidh and many others who fell that day. The exact details of their conversion are not unknown. Can anyone say that the filth of their souls and the evil of their hearts were cleansed by the blade of a sword?

The three great Companions who later fought so valiantly to defend the faith were Sad b. Abi Waqqas, Abu Ubaydah b. al-Jarrah and Khalid b. Walid. None was converted to Islam by force. Hundreds of Emigrants (Muhajirun) and thousands of Helpers (Ansar) were converted and gave the persecuted Prophet[sa] sanctuary. No sword was involved in their conversion. These converts were the fruits of Islam, the pride of mankind, the signposts on the path to ultimate truth. What greater insult to them than to say their hearts were purified by the sword, or to suggest that it was 'fallacious to say that the sword did not play any role in [their] conversion'?

What were these people before the advent of Islam? Before Muhammad[sa], Arabia existed as a political unit only, as Will Durant pointed out. He said: 'In the careless nomenclature of the Greeks, who called all the population of the peninsula *Sarakenoi* ('Saracens), apparently from the Arabic *sharqiun*, "easterners".'[7] Previously they were called 'Scenite Arabs' - Arabs who lived in tents (from the Greek word *skene*, a tent. They lived in an arid land and communication problems meant there was tribal self-sufficiency. During the second millenium before the Christian era, the Arabs domesticated the camel, an animal perfectly suited to the desert. It provided milk for sustenance and urine for medicinal use. Its meat was tender and its hide and hair made tents and clothing. Even its dung could be used for fuel. It could go for twenty-five days in winter without water and five in summer. Small groups of nomads followed the camels, the camels being their most important resource. Aloy Sprenger summed up the whole pre-Islamic Saracen history by describing the Arabs as the 'camel's parasites'.

> The Arab felt no duty of loyalty to any group larger than his own tribe, but the intensity of his devotion varied inversely to its extent; for his tribe, he would do with conscience what civilised people do only for their country, religion or race - i.e., lie, steal, kill and die.[8]

He was bound by no written laws and no state existed to enforce the law.

23

Arabs mourned the birth of daughters and hid their faces in shame. Sometimes daughters were killed at birth. If they survived, their natural charm might earn them a few years of love from husbands and lovers who would go to the ends of the earth to defend their honour. But they were no more than pieces of property. They were part of the estate of their fathers, husbands or sons and were bequeathed with other belongings. They were also slaves, rarely friends of their fathers, husbands or brothers.

The Arab gave scant thought to life after death. He offered human sacrifice; he worshipped 'sacred' stones. The centre of this stone worship was Mecca. In pre-Muslim days, within the Kaba, were several idols supposed to represent gods. The great god of Mecca was Hubal, an idol made of cornelian. But in the Hijaz, three goddesses - Lat, Manat and Uzza - had pride of place as the daughters of God.

Well-built and strong, the Arab could live on just a few dates and some camel's milk. From the date palm he made a wine which raised him up into poetic flights of imagination and romance. His life alternated between loving and fighting and he was quick to avenge insult and injury, not only for himself but also on his tribe's behalf.

An eye for an eye and a tooth for a tooth was the law. Never-ending shame awaited an avenger if he could not kill his tormentor. A large part of his life was spent in tribal vendetta (Arabic *tha'r*). In the pre-Islamic Arab history *Ayyam ul-Arab*, (Days of the Arabs), was the name applied to the battles the Arabs fought among themselves. Particular days were called, for example, Day of Buath or Days of al-Fijar. These inter-tribal hostilities generally sprang from disputes over cattle, land or springs. One of the most famous was fought between the Banu-Bakr and their kinsmen the Banu-Taghlib over a she-camel, owned by an old woman from Bakr called Basus. A Taghlib chief had wounded the camel . . . the resulting war lasted forty years! It ended only when both tribes had exhausted each other. Another famous war was the Day of Dahis and Al-Ghabra, which erupted over the unfair conduct of two chieftains in a race between a horse (named Dahis) and a mare (called Al-Ghabra). War broke out soon after the Basus conflict ended and continued at invervals for several decades.

This was the social background in which Muhammad[sa] was brought up and these were the people whom God gave the first opportunity of embracing a persecuted prophet's faith.

To suggest that these fierce and warlike people - who would sound the battle cry at the drop of a hat - could have been converted by force is to contradict history. Moreover, it demeans the faith of those pioneers who put their lives at stake to defend Islam at the battle of Badr.

Usayd b. Hudayr, Sad b. Khaythamah, Asd b. Zurahah, Abdullah b. Rawahah, Sad b. Ubadah, Mundhir b. Amir, Bara b. Marur, Ubadah b. as-Sami, Rafi b. Malik and many other Helpers travelled all the way from Medina to Mecca to embrace Islam. Even to hint that the sword played a part in their conversion is also to deny historical fact.

While in Christian history it is religion which converts swords into ploughshares,[9] Maulana Maududi's interpretation of Islamic history asks us to believe it is the sword which prepares the soil of the soul to receive religion's seed.[10] Was it the Holy Prophet's[sa] sword or a few verses of the Holy Quran which turned Umar b. Khattab - a sworn enemy of Islam - into Islam's devoted servant?

In the early days of the Prophet's[sa] persecution, Umar, a headstrong young man of 26, decided to kill the Prophet[sa], thus wiping out the main cause of division among the Quraysh. On his way to the Prophet's[sa] house, he met Nuaim b. Abdullah, who sensed his evil intentions and said: 'O Umar! Go back to the people of thy house! Thy sister, Fatima, and thy brother-in-law, Saeed, have embraced the religion of Muhammad.' And, without a single word, Umar went straight to his sister's house, where a Companion, Khabbab, was reciting the opening verses of the Surah, Ta-Ha (XX). As soon as Umar went in, Khabbab hid in a corner and Fatima hid the pages of the Quran in her clothing. But Umar had overheard Khabbab's recital and attacked both Saeed and Fatima. When Fatima was covered in blood, he softened and asked to see the verses. He read them and exclaimed: 'How beautiful and how noble these words are!' And he went straight to Arqam's house, where the Prophet[sa] was sitting with his Companions. He cried out: 'O Messenger of Allah! I have come to thee that I may declare my faith in Allah and His Messenger and in what he hath brought from Allah.'

Why is Maulana Maududi so determined to paint a violent picture of Islam? Why are there contradictions in his theory of *jihad*? A glance at the Maulana's background and the conditions under which he wrote his book, *Al-Jihad fil Islam*, can help us answer these questions.

Syed Abul Ala-Maududi spent his childhood and early youth in Hyderabad (Deccan) where the Nizam still ruled in the style of the great Mughal and where his Hindu prime minister sang the praises of the Holy

Prophet[sa].[11] At the crossroads, from north to south and east to west, it was the last stronghold of Mughal - predominantly Muslim - culture in India. In a state where the population was overwhelmingly Hindu (more than 80 per cent) and Muslims were a small minority (just 10 per cent), the ruler though without effective power, still recalled the past glory of Mughal rule. It was an unreal world. The court, with its Paigah nobility, chamberlains, household troops, brocade *sherwanis*, ceremonial *dastar* (turban), *bugloos* (buckle) and gorgeous jewellery, was a reminder of the Delhi Court before it was ravaged by Nadir Shah (1739). There were Arab mercenaries with gilded daggers and long muskets and the regular army with all the paraphernalia of modern warfare. The rajas and maharajahs - some of them reigning over areas larger than the Hindu states of British India - occupied the highest places of honour in the Nizam's government and were part of a surreal picture of Muslim tolerance and Hindu loyalty.

Though the Hyderabadi culture was recognisably Indian based, it was largely Muslim in shape. 'Social organisation was still feudal, but not in any sense primitive. It was highly cultivated with a grace of manner, and, above all, a tolerance and mutual respect which could speak volumes to our generation if we could listen.[12]

It was in this Hyderabad that the young Maududi's personality was formed.[13] Sensitive and impressionable, he started his journalistic career in 1918 by joining the editorial staff of the *Medina* (Bijnore). After working as editor of the *Taj* (Jabalpur) he took over the editorship of *Al-Jamiyat* (Delhi) in 1925. The *shuddi* movement was at its height and, as mentioned earlier, at this time the young editor of *Al-Jamiyat* started writing his articles. They were obviously written under the pressure of his day-to-day work and they were all completed within six months.[14] Maududi began to write these articles 'more as a nationalist than a religious zealot', but on further study of Islamic literature - as much as he could read in six months and without Islamic schooling - he became a religious revivalist.[15] Both his articles in *Al-Jihad fil Islam* and the overall evolution of his own thought were very much peacemeal. He started writing the book as a nationalist Indian[16] and, as such, his aim was to prove to the Indian Hindus, and especially to Gandhiji, that Islam was not a religion of violence. In a speech at Jami Masjid, Delhi, the great Indian Muslim leader, Maulana Muhammad Ali Jowhar, said he wished that a Muslim would write a book pointing out that Islam had nothing to do with violence. Young Maududi was among the audience and decided to take up the task.[17] So, in the first instalments of his articles, he pointed out to Hindus that Islam was not a religion of the sword. But our author was born and bred in a Muslim kingdom where the Hindu majority was under a Muslim leader.

The writer of two books on the history of Hyderabad[18] was steeped in the power of political authority. He soon contradicted his own arguments against the *jihad* of the sword. This Hyderabadi Muslim was to assert: 'It is fallacious to say that the sword did not play any role in conversion.' The young journalist was neither a historian nor a scholar of religion. He could not understand that though Muslim dynasties ruled the Deccan for 600 years, the overwhelming majority of that area remained Hindu. Political power in Muslim hands has never helped conversion to Islam. The author of *Jihad fil Islam* was just 24 years old. And the Maulana, even at the age of 65, remained 'superficial'. As Prof. Fazlur Rahman observed:

> Maududi, though not an *alim*, was nevertheless a self-taught man of considerable intelligence and sufficient knowledge. . . . He was by no means an accurate or profound scholar, but he was undoubtedly like a fresh wind in the stifling Islamic atmosphere created by the traditional madrasas. . . . But Maududi displays nowhere the larger and more profound vision of Islam's role in the world. Being a journalist rather than a serious scholar he wrote at great speed and with resultant superficiality in order to feed his eager young readers - and he wrote incessantly. . . . Not one of Maududi's followers ever became a serious student of Islam, the result being that, for the faithful, Maududi's statements represented the last word on Islam - no matter how much *and how blatantly he contradicted himself* from time to time on such basic issues as economic policy and political theory.[19]

The late Mufti Kifayatullah of Delhi held the same opinion. He said: 'I know Maulana Abul Ala Maududi. He has neither learned from nor been disciplined by a scholar of repute. He is very well read *but his understanding of religion is weak.*[20]

The late Maulana Husain Ahmad Madani foresaw the danger very clearly and said:

> His pamphlets and books contain opinions which are anti-religious and heretic, though written with theological trappings. Lay readers cannot see through these trappings. As a result they find the Islam brought by the Holy Prophet repugnant; the Islam which has been followed by the Ummat-i-Muhammadiya for the last 1350 years.[21]

In one of his letters, Maualana Qari Muhammad Tayyab wrote:

'Having read Maududi Sahib's writings I have concluded that he did not acquire the disciplines of Muslim legal philosophy and mysticism. He cannot write on them with authority.[22]

The late Maulana Ahmad Ali Lahauri also wrote in the same vein:

Maududi Sahib wants to present a 'New Islam' to the Muslims. And Muslims will not accept a 'New Islam' unless the old Islam, which they have followed for the last 1,350 years, is not fully destroyed and it is proved that Islam has become irrelevant and impractical.[23]

Maulana Maududi, as we have seen, was neither an historian nor a religious scholar. he was essentially a journalist and he had the two basic qualities of a journalist: a good command of the Urdu language and the ability to write quickly. The *Al-Jamiyat* was a bi-weekly at that time and he had to write his column on *jihad* within two or three days, in addition to editing his newspaper. Having no background in research and no time for it then, he mistook the battle of Hunayn (30 January 630), which came soon after the submission of Mecca (11 January), as a turning-point in Islamic history. Since Islam's enemies were decisively beaten at Hunayn, the Maulana concluded that it was this victory and the political power gained through it which helped the conversion of the whole of Arabia to Islam. Maulana Maududi is not alone in drawing this conclusion. The orientalists, who see no moral or spiritual force in Islamic teachings and are unable to understand the great miracles performed by our Holy Prophet,[sa] have always put Muslim expansion down to force. The orientalists divided the life of the Prophet[sa] into two sections, the first the period of Meccan persecution and second the period of conquest after his migration to Medina. Our young journalist, Abul Ala Maududi, with his superficial knowledge of Islamic history, accepted this apparently simplistic but, in reality, very clever division of the Holy Prophet's[sa] life.

Armed conflict, war and threats of war were forced constantly on the Prophet.[sa] After he migrated to Medina, the pagans of Mecca and the Jews of Medina, encouraged by the hypocrites, busily plotted against Islam. They inspired hatred against Muslims and worked pagan Arabs up to a fever pitch against the Holy Prophet[sa]. All the defensive actions the Muslims were forced to take obstructed the Prophet's[sa] basic mission. Muslims needed peace but, as our examination will show, that peace was deliberately disturbed to prevent them from spreading the new faith.

1 Islam's enemies used every means of communication against Islam. For the Arabs, poets were historians, genealogists, satirists, moralists and

founts of wisdom.[24] The poet was the 'kindler of battle'[25] and 'the journalist of the time'.[26] The Ansar (the Muslims of Medina) were accused of dishonouring themselves by submitting to an outsider. Asma bint Marwan of Umayyah b. Zayd composed verses taunting and insulting Medinite Muslims. She said:

Cowards[27] of Malik and Nabit
And cowards of Awf and Khazraj
You obey a stranger who does not belong to you
Who is neither a Murad nor a Mad'hij[28]
Do you - when your own chiefs have
been murdered - hope in him
Like the greedy people looking towards
a cooking pot of meal soup?
Is there no man of honour among you who will
take advantage of an unguarded moment
And cut off the gulls' hopes?[29]

The centenarian poet of Khazrajite class, Abu Afak, taunted the Medinites with the following verses:

I have lived a long time, but I have
never seen
Either a house or gathering of people
More loyal and faithful to
Its allies, when they call on them,
Than those of the Children of Qayla[30]
as a whole.
The mountains will crumble before they submit.
Yet here is a rider come among them
who has divided them.
(He says) 'This is permitted, this is
forbidden'
To all kinds of things
But if you had believed in power
And in might, why did you not follow
Tubba?[31]

Tubbas were south Arabian kings of great reputation. Abu Afak, in effect, asked the Ansar, 'Once you resisted Tubba, now what has happened to you that you have accepted the claims of a Meccan refugee?' While Asma and Abu Afak were putting the Ansar to shame, the Jewish poet Kab b. al-Ashraf[32], enraged by the Muslim victory at Badr, went all the way to Mecca to rouse the Quraish against the Holy Prophet[sa]. He played on the Arab weakness for vengeance:

29

Badr's mill ground out the blood of its people.
At events like Badr you should weep and cry.
The best people were killed round their cisterns.
Don't think it strange that princes were left lying
How many noble, handsome men,
The refuge of the homeless, were slain,
Liberal when the stars gave no rain.[33]

2 The vendetta, as we have observed earlier, was one of the pillars of pre-Islamic Arab society. So, whenever a pagan combatant was killed by a Muslim in armed conflict, his heirs took an oath to avenge his death and the whole tribe accused Islam of his death. The fact that conflicts were initiated by pagans themselves was conveniently forgotten.

3 The Holy Prophet's[sa] mission was restricted to a small area of Arabia because of the general hostility to him. Missionaries could not take the message of Islam to the whole of the peninsula.

4 Many Arabs had accepted Islam, but fear of war made them afraid to declare their new faith.

5 Conversion to a new religion requires commitment and courage, even when honour and life itself are not at risk. Here, acceptance of Islam demanded more than the joining of a religious society: it meant taking up arms in its defence. Since Muslims at this time were unarmed and weak, it was suicide to join them.

6 Self-defence kept the Muslims so busy that very little time was left for spreading the faith.

If our premise is correct, the ending of hostilities should have immediately boosted the spread of Islam. As we shall see, this is exactly what happened. Mecca was conquered in January 630. That, according to the orientalists and enemies of Islam, was the turning-point in Islamic history. If that were true, one could indeed say that the sword had played a role in the spread of Islam. But history tells a rather different story. Hostilities between the Muslims and the pagan Arabs ended with the truce of Al-Hudaybiah[34] (March 628). The terms of the truce appeared to be so degrading that 'Umar could not contain himself, and asked the Prophet[sa]: 'Why yield we in such lowly wise against the honour of our

30

religion?' The Meccans thought it was a victory. But it was this respite from armed conflict which gave the Holy Prophet[sa] much more time to spread the faith. The extent of his success can be gauged by the number of people who marched to Mecca with him in January 630. Previously, his largest force had been 3000 men. This was the strength of the Muslim army which defended Medina when it was besieged by an army of 10,000 pagan Arabs.[35] The additional 7000 men were obviously converted to Islam during the two-year truce. People like Amr b. al-As and Khalid b. Walid were converted at this time. The success of this peaceful penetration by Islam was so great that a puzzled Montgomery Watt counts it 'among the imponderabilia' and adds: 'Foremost among the reasons for this success of Muhammad's was the attractiveness of Islam and its relevance as a religious and social system to the religious and social needs of the Arabs.'[36] Watt also says, as if directly addressing Maulana Maududi himself:

> Had Muhammad not been able to maintain and strengthen his hold on the Muslims by the sway of religious ideas of Islam over their imaginations, and had he not been able to attract fresh converts to Islam, the treaty of Al-Hudaybiah would not have worked in his favour. . . . Any historian who is not biased in favour of materialism must also allow as factors of supreme importance Muhammad's belief in the message of the Quran, his belief in the structure of Islam as a religious and political system, and his unflinching devotion to the task to which, as he believed, God had called him . . . This expedition and treaty mark a new initiative on the part of Muhammad.[37]

It is sad to note that while an orientalist puts the Holy Prophet's[sa] success down to 'the sway of the religious ideas of Islam', a leading Muslim of Maulana Maududi's stature insists that it was through the sway of the sword after the battle of Hunayn that teeming thousands of Arabs accepted Islam. If these were the people whose souls were cleansed with the blade of the sword, then these were also the people who were the first to revolt after the Prophet's[sa] death. That answer to the Maulana's argument, however, does not explain the revolt.

In the past travel was difficult. There were no roads and therefore one's safety could not be guaranteed. It was, therefore, impossible for every Arab to come to the Prophet[sa] to learn about Islam at first hand, nor for the Prophet to visit every region of the peninsula. The Arab custom was that either a tribal delegation would be sent to the Prophet[sa] or a Muslim delegation would be sent to the tribes to deliver the message of Islam. There were discussions and debates, and after every question had been asked the tribe accepted whatever the members of the delegation or the elders of the tribe decided. So there was a large number of converts who had no opportunity of benefiting directly from the Prophet's[sa] teaching; they had never even seen him. They did not even have the chance to spend time with the Prophet's[sa] Companions. Religion is a personal experience and is learned especially by example and inspiration, things not available to the new converts. Misfortune was compounded by the death of the Holy Prophet[sa] soon after their conversion. The Arab horizon was more than a little darkened by the passing away of Muhammad[sa]. We can learn a great deal from that period of history. When people reject the prophet of their time and extinguish his light by force, they are severely punished for it.

One result of that punishment is that most people see the light of *iman* (belief) when the source of that light is about to be extinguished. Sometimes people only recognise a prophet long after his death. What a punishment! To persecute a prophet while he is alive; to accept him only after he has gone.

Since Maulana Maududi joined the worst enemies of Islam by arguing that the sword played a part in the preaching of Islam, let us re-examine the Prophet's[sa] life to see if at any stage people were converted against their will.

The division of the Holy Prophet's[sa] life into two periods, the Meccan and the Medinite, seems logical, but it is in reality an over-simplification. After the Hijrah, the Prophet[sa] and the Emigrants had escaped persecution, but the struggle for survival was not over. It would be more logical to divide the Prophet's[sa] life into three phases: the first being the time up to his migration to Medina, and the second the time from his migration to the truce of Hudaybiyah, which was also a period of persecution; the third from the truce to the surrender of Mecca. (Though the Muslims were allowed to fight back, they were no match for the pagan opposition. Medina was the only town where Muslims lived, but they did not control it. The three Jewish tribes and the non-Muslim members of the Aws and the Khazraj dominated the town. The size of the opposing armies at the battle of Badr[38] represented their actual strength. Therefore, this period should be considered an extension of the Meccan period of bitter struggle.) The third period begins with the truce of Hudaybiyah and ends with the surrender of Mecca. It was a period of peace. The Meccan pagans did not attack the Muslims, though a few skirmishes took place with the Jews and some Arab tribes who broke their agreements with the Muslims.

The first period of persecution lasted thirteen years. During that time there was no question of conversion by force. Even the orientalists agree with that. In fact, people accepted Islam in spite of Meccan persecution. Muslims who accepted Islam in Mecca at that time are known as *Muhajirs* (Emigrants) and it is an historical fact that no Emigrant was unwillingly converted.

The Muslims offered armed resistance during the second period of their persecution. A critic might think that during that armed conflict at least some might have been forced into accepting Islam. But the history of the period is fully documented. The majority of Muslims in Medina belonged to two Arab tribes, the Aws and the Khazraj. These were the people who had invited the Holy Prophet[sa] to Medina. When they met him at Aqbah, he said: 'I make with you this pact on condition that the allegiance you pledge me shall bind you to protect me even as you protect your women and children.' The Khazrajite chief, Bara, who rose to reply, took the Prophet's[sa] hand and said:

By Him who sent thee with the truth, we will protect thee as we protect them. So accept the pledge of our allegiance, O Messenger of God, for we are men of war, possessed of arms that have been handed down from father to son.

These were the people who travelled all the way from Yathrib (Medina) to Mecca to offer their swords to the Prophet[sa] and who are now known as Ansar (Helpers).

A few Jews in Medina and a small number of Arabs from outlying towns also became Muslims, but none of them accepted their new faith under duress or as a result of armed conflict. During this period the spread of Islam in Mecca was relentless and, despite greater persecution, the Meccan Arabs continued to accept Islam. Again, force did not enter into it.

The conversion of prisioners-of-war is the only remotely possible exception. Before we look at it, let us clear up one misunderstanding. The words *ghazwah* and *sariyah* do not mean 'war' or even 'armed conflict'. They only mean 'an expedition'. Scouts, patrols, embassies, rescue parties, the chasing of highwaymen - even a single Companion's journey to preach - are grouped under these titles. Expeditions were known as *sariyah*; if the Prophet[sa] himself led them, as *ghazwah*. For instance, the first expedition the Prophet[sa] led was to Al-Abwa, where his mother was buried. He was accompanied by sixty Muhajirs. The Holy Prophet[sa] stayed there for a few days and signed a treaty of friendship with the chief of the Bunu Damrah. Soon after, the Prophet[sa] had to follow Kurz al-Fihri. As Watt points out, 'It was an attempt to punish a freebooter of the neighbouring region for stealing some of the Medinite pasturing camels.'[39] The expedition, again in the words of Watt, 'Illustrates the dangers against which he [the Holy Prophet[sa]] had to be constantly on guard.'[40] There were about fifty such expeditions between Hijrah and the truce of Hudaybiyah. Of them, three conflicts assumed the dimensions of full-scale war: Badr, Uhud and Ahzab. In the armed conflict with B. Mustaliq over 100 prisoners were taken, but all of them were freed without ransom. In some minor expeditions where one or two prisoners were seized, they too were released without any conditions. It was at the battle of Badr that seventy-two prisoners-of-war were taken. Two of them were executed for past crimes; the rest were freed after a ransom was paid. That, in some cases, was limited only to teaching the children of Ansar how to read and write.

The third period began with the truce of Hudaybiyah and ended with the surrender of Mecca. Twenty-two expeditions were made during this period. Of them, only three conflicts saw any prisoners-of-war being taken. The Prophet[sa] had sent Dihyah b. Khalifah al-Kalbi as an envoy to Caesar. On his return journey, Dihyah was robbed of Byzantine presents he was carrying for the Holy Prophet[sa], by Al-Hunayd and other members of the tribe of Jurham. The Prophet[sa] sent an expedition under Zayd b. Haritha to punish Al-Hunayd and his allies. The prisoners taken in the resulting skirmish were freed after they repented. Bashir b. Sad successfully led an expedition against the Ghatfan, who were in alliance with the Jews of Medina and the pagans of Mecca. A small number of prisioners were taken, but it is not known what happened to them. Similarly, an expedition was sent to punish B. Bani Kilab. A group of B. Uraynah, who lived among the B. Kilab, came in distress to Medina and accepted Islam. As they were suffering from a fever, they were sent to the Prophet's[sa] pasture grounds to enjoy good food and milk. But, when they recovered their strength, they cruelly killed the herdsmen and stole fifteen camels. They were punished. There was probably a small number of prisoners, but the details are not known.

This rather detailed examination shows that from the Hijrah to the surrender of Mecca, not a single prisoner-of-war was forced to convert. There is no evidence to suggest that the filth of their soul was removed by the blade of the sword. Rather, these prisoners were allowed to return to their paganism.

The final period of the Holy Prophet's[sa] life began with Mecca's surrender - or the day of the conquering of hearts. That Islamic victory over the Meccans conclusively proved that the spreading of Islam was not even remotely connected with violence. Not one person was converted by force.

Abu Sufyan, the arch-enemy of Islam, who became a Muslim on the eve of the Prophet's[sa] triumphant entry into Mecca, watched the Muslim army from a vantage point near the city. The Holy Prophet's[sa] uncle, Abbas, was with him. What Abu Sufyan saw there has been vividly described by Martin Lings:

> Troop after troop went by, and, at the passing of each, Abu Sufyan asked who they were, and each time he marvelled, either because the tribe in question had hitherto been far beyond the range of influence of Quraish, or because it had recently been hostile to the Prophet, as was the case with the Ghatafanite clan of Ashja, one of whose ensigns was borne by Nuaym, the former friend of himself and Suhayl.
>
> 'Of all the Arabs,' said Abu Sufayn, 'These were Muhammad's bitterest foes.'
>
> 'God caused Islam to enter their hearts,' said Abbas. 'All this is by the grace of God.'[41]

Was it the sword which converted them? And when the Prophet[sa] entered Mecca with his 10,000 men, did he avenge the thirteen-year persecution? The idea of settling scores was certainly in the minds of some. When Sad ibn Ubada saw Abu Sufyan he said: 'O Abu Sufyan, this is the day of slaughter: the day when the inviolable shall be violated: the day of God's abasement of Quraish.' When Abu Sufyan repeated to the Holy Prophet[sa] what Sad had said, the Prophet[sa] replied: 'This is the day of mercy, the day on which God has exalted Quraish.' A general amnesty was proclaimed. Using the words of Joseph[as], as reported in the Quran, Muhammad[sa] said: 'Verily I say as my brother Joseph said, this day there shall be no reproach on you. May Allah forgive you. He is the Most Merciful of all those who show mercy.' (12.93)

Washington Irving, by no means a sympathetic observer of Islam, describes the Holy Prophet's[sa] entry into Mecca in the following way:

> The sun was just rising as he entered the gates of his native city, with the glory of a conqueror, but the garb and humility of a pilgrim. He entered, repeating verses of the Koran, which he said had been revealed to him at Medina, and were prophetic of the event. He triumphed in the spirit of a religious zealot, *not a warrior*.[42]

Meccan leaders who opposed the Prophet[sa] with every means at their disposal were not only magnanimously pardoned but also, as even Montgomery Watt admits: 'Were not forced to become Muslims; they and doubtless many others remained pagan, at least till after Al-Jiranah'.[43] Maxime Rodinson agrees with Watt: 'No man seems to have felt under constraint to embrace Islam.'[44]

Had there been even the remotest hint of conversion by force in our primary sources of *hadith* or *sirah*, the critics of Islam would have had a field day. Now compare again the opinions of Irving, Watt and Rodinson with what Maulana Maududi said on the subject: 'When every method of persuasion failed, the Prophet[sa] took to the sword. That sword removed evil and mischief and the filth of the soul.'

The conquest of Mecca will be engraved on the pages of history for ever. That day will continue to absolve the Prophet[sa] - the Mercy for Mankind - from charges of violence and force which Maulana Maududi has imputed to him. That a non-Muslim orientalist, Stanley Lane-Poole, should have to put right Maududi's mistake is a tragedy of great magnitude which should sadden the heart of every Muslim. Lane-Poole says:

> The day of Muhammad's greatest triumph over his enemies was also the day of his grandest victory over himself. He freely forgave the Quraish all the years of sorrow and cruel scorn to which they had inflicted him, and gave an amnesty to the whole population of Mecca.[45]

The last phase of the Prophet's[sa] life begins with Mecca's conquest and ends with his death. There were seven expeditions during this time. There was no fighting at all in three of them and no prisoners were taken. In the remaining four, more than 6000 prisoners were seized. And just what happened to these prisoners? Maududi's logic would lead us to believe that this would have been the perfect occasion for removing filth from prisoners' souls and converting them to Islam. History tells us something different.

At the battle of Hunayn, 6000 prisoners were taken. The Holy Prophet[sa] had spent his infancy with one of the clans of this tribe as a foster child. Among the prisoners, an old woman protested to her captor saying, 'By God, I am the sister of your chief!' The woman was produced before the Holy Prophet[sa], who realised it was indeed one of his foster-sisters, Shayma'. The Prophet[sa] spread his rug and bade her be seated. With tears in his eyes he asked about Halimah, his foster-mother. There was no word of reproach. The Prophet[sa] did not ask why the tribe had not thought of its foster-son before going to war. Instead, he said: 'So far those who have fallen unto me and unto the sons of Abd ul-Muttalib, they are yours; and

I will plead with other men on your behalf.' When other Muslims heard about this they said: 'What belongs to us, belongs to the Holy Prophet[sa]', and they immediately presented their captives to him. Thus all 6000 prisoners were freed. The sword played no part in their conversion. The Holy Prophet[sa] gave his foster-sister camels, sheep and goats as presents. Harith, the brother of the Holy Prophet's[sa] foster-father, insisted that the whole tribe of Hawazin be considered his foster-kinsmen. Their leader, Malik, who had escaped to Taif, was recalled and given 100 camels. The Holy Prophet[sa] also put him in command of the already increasing Muslim community in Hawazin. Many others also received gifts.

Similarly, sixty-two prisoners were brought to Medina from the expedition of Uyaynah b. Hisn. They asked for mercy and were released.

In the expedition to Fuls, a centre of idol worship, Adi, the leader of the opposing tribe, Tayy, escaped but one of his sisters was captured. When she was brought to Medina she threw herself at the Prophet's[sa] feet and begged for mercy. She said: 'My father freed the prisoners, provided hospitality for guests, fed the hungry and gave comfort to those in distress. He never turned away anyone who came to his door seeking help. I am the daughter of Hatim.'

The Holy Prophet[sa] spoke kindly to her and ordered her release, saying: 'Her father loved noble ways, and Allah likewise loves them.' The Prophet gave her a camel and fine garments. Since she did not want to be released alone, all other captives taken with her were also freed. All this was done because she was the daughter of a great poet, whose hospitality and generosity made Arabs proud. When Adi heard of his sister's treatment he entered Islam and the Holy Prophet[sa] confirmed his chieftancy of Tayy.

Surveying the orientalists' conflicting opinions about the Prophet's personality, Maxime Rodinson has observed: 'Everyone has shaped him after their own passions, ideas or fantasies.'[46] This observation applies more to Maulana Maududi, a Muslim, than it does to non-Muslim orientalists. His passion for political authority was fed on his childhood impressions of fading Hyderabadi glory and strengthened by the political struggle of his younger days, when he first admired Gandhiji and then opposed Hindu communalism. This so dominated his thinking that in his account he converted the life of the Holy Prophet[sa] - a blessing for all mankind - into that of a warrior . . . a warrior putting the world to rights with the blade of a sword.

CHAPTER 4

PROPHETS AND TROOPERS
A Study in Contrast

Remind them for thou (O Prophet) art an admonisher. Thou art not at all a warder over them.

Quran, 82.22 - 3

It [Jamaati Islami] is not a missionary organisation or a body of preachers or evangelists, but an organisation of God's troopers.

Maulana Abul Ala Maududi[1]

The picture of Muhammad, the Prophet of Islam[sa] painted by nineteenth-century orientalists has been examined in the previous chapter. It was a picture of a fanatical warrior riding out of the Arabian deserts with a drawn sword in one hand and the Quran in the other, offering his helpless victims a choice between the two. The harshness of this picture, popularised by Edward Gibbon[2] has now been toned down by modern orientalists. Even the well-known Jewish scholar, Bernard Lewis, with his dry British humour, had to admit that the picture, 'Is not only false but also impossible - unless we are able to assume a race of left-handed swordsmen. In Muslim practice, the left hand is reserved for unclean purposes, and no self-respecting Muslim would use it to raise the Quran.'[3]

But there is one 'self-respecting' Muslim, Maulana Maududi, who clutched his drawn sword in his right hand, irrespective of its lack of relevance to the teachings of the Holy Quran and the practices of the Holy Prophet[sa].

The Maulana claims to be a loyal follower of the Prophet[sa], and, as such, one would expect him to talk admiringly of his Master. Beauty is in the eye of the beholder. But how can he see defects in his Lord which even Islam's modern enemies reject? There are three answers to this question.

1 That the Maulana's claim to be a loyal follower of Islam is false. In view

of what the Maulana wrote in *Al-Jihad fiil Islam* and his other works, the reader may reasonably be led to believe that the author is not even remotely concerned with the teachings of the Holy Prophet[sa] and that his claim to be a loyal follower is false. That would be a very serious charge. Since I belong to a sect which has been falsely accused of showing disrespect to the Holy Prophet[sa], I would be the last to doubt the Maulana's loyalty to our Lord and Master, Muhammad - may Allah bless him and grant him peace.

2 That the Maulana's sense of values has been confused, so he has as much difficulty in telling good from evil as a colour-blind person does in telling red from green.

3 That the Maulana is obsessed - obsessed with a desire for political power and authority. Obsession has been defined as 'A persistent or recurrent idea, usually strongly tinged with emotion, frequently involving an urge towards some form of action; the whole mental situation being pathological.'[4]

Pierre Janet found that an obsessive person was scrupulous, ever-conscientious and stricken by a sense of worthlessness.[5] Elton Mayo has summarised Janet's and his own characterisation of obsessives in these terms: 'They are the experts in arduous rethinking of the obvious - they substitute an exaggerated precision in minor activities for that activity in major affairs *of which they are or feel themselves to be incapable.*[6]

The Maulana's childhood memories and adolescent experiences in Hyderabad, as we have seen earlier, led him towards one source of behavioural control - political power. Kurt Lewin has observed that if an individual's behaviour is to be understood, it must be in terms of his life-space - one has to relate the individual to his environment over the course of time and *at the particular moment*. Lewin's field of interest is thus: 'the life-space, containing the person and his psychological environment.'[7] Woodsworth and Sheehan elaborate Lewin's theory and say:

The psychological (or behavioural) environment is, of course, the environment as perceived and understood by the person, but more than that, it is the environment as related to his present needs and quasi-needs. Many objects which are perceived are of no present concern to him and so exist only in the background of his psychological environment. Other objects have positive or negative 'valence' - positive if they promise to meet his present needs, negative if they threaten injury. Objects of positive valence attract him, while objects of negative valence repel him.[8]

39

Psychology is not an absolute science and it is still evolving, but Maulana Maududi's 'obsession' seems to fit the theory we have discussed. That is not to say, of course, that there might not be another explanation of his obsessive behaviour. Whatever the explanation, the Maulana's vision has undoubtedly been blurred by obsession. He trips and, at times, stumbles into paths which have been traversed before him by the enemies of God. It is this obsession which causes him to support capital punishment for those who switch religions.[9] This punishment has always been demanded for prophets and their followers who change from their traditional religion. It is the same obsession which impels him to put a sword into the Holy Prophet's[sa] hand and, in doing so, to support those enemies of Islam who paint a gory picture of Muhannad[sa]. Since persuasion and force are mutually exclusive, the Maulana adopts the sword as a means of reform and rejects reasoning as a method of conversion. Persuasion and reasoning are difficult tasks of which he is or feels himself to be incapable. They entail sacrifice and long suffering in the face of opposition, as the Prophet's[sa] Meccan life showed. So the Maulana rejects them as objects of negative valence. Force through political power seems to meet his present needs, so he adopts it and relates it to the Holy Prophet's[sa] life with a process of arduous thinking.

When I refer to the Maulana's obsession, I do not mean to show him any disrespect, although, by putting a sword into the hands of my Lord and Master Muhammad[sa] he has shown disrespect to the Prophet[sa] and all he stood for. Reviewing Israel Shenker's book, *Coat of Many Colors*, a collection of essays on Judaism, Hugh Nissenden says: 'Mr Shenker dramatises his obsession in a way that makes the history of his people accessible and illuminating to everyone.'[10] I only wish the Maulana could put his obsession to good use. Instead, he justifies force, not only as legitimate, but also as an essential method of reform. He says: 'It is not possible that they [the enemies of Islam] would sacrifice their interests in the face of persuasion and reasoning. All that one can do is to acquire political power[11] and force them to stop their mischief.'[12]

This method of reform seems to be effective and also easier than persuasion, which requires patience and persistence in the face of ridicule, rebuffs and snubs. It is so easy to convert people by force. There is no comparison between the two methods. One is easy and quick; the other difficult and time consuming, requiring the patience of Job[as]. All reformers have had to endure ridicule and rejection. This is how the Quran describes their lot:

Those who were guilty used to laugh at those who believed; and when they passed by them, they winked at each other. When they came back to their families, they exulted over them; and when they saw them they exclaimed: 'These indeed are the lost ones.' But they were not appointed keepers over them. (83.30-4)

The verses quoted above explain why the Maulana would not follow the path of the reformers sent by God. People laugh at reformers and say: 'Look at these people whose only weapon is persuasion! They are so weak we can crush them whenever we wish; and yet they claim to win people over by their reasoning and advice.' So the Maulana rejected peaceful argument and said instead:

Anyone who wants to uproot mischief and disorder from this world and wants to reform mankind should realise that he cannot do so by mere sermonising and counselling. It is useless. He should rise against the government of false principles, he should seize power, remove the wrongdoers from authority and set up a government based on sound principles and just administration.[13]

But the Maududian method of reform, which is modelled on Marxism, is not the divine way of saving mankind. In God's plan, persuasion is so important that, even in an age of general moral decline, only pious believers 'who exhort one another with truth and steadfastness' (103.4) will succeed. Even a cursory glance at history will reveal that for spiritual and moral revolutions God asks his servants to win over the people with truth and patience. Patience and prayer are the integral part of religious revolution and they should continue to be exhorted till God's promise is fulfilled. It is foretold that 'the [pleasing] end is for the righteous'. (7.129)

All God's messengers have followed this method of religious reform, one which is totally opposed to the Marxist use of force. The Quran preserves the account of many prophets and evangelists. According to this divine account, Noah's[as] instrument of revolution was persuasion and Abraham's[as] was also. It was the instrument of Shuaib[as] and Saleh[as]. Lot[as] was also sent as a counsellor and so was Moses[as]. Jesus[as] caused a revolution with his sermons. And, above all, the Seal of the Prophets, the leading reformer of all time, our Master Muhammad[sa] was sent to bring about a universal spiritual revolution with nothing but persuasion and reasoning. But the Maulana not only ignores this tradition of God's holy messengers; he also contradicts it in the following words: 'Anyone who wants to uproot mischief and disorder from this world and wants to reform mankind should realise that he cannot do so by mere sermonising and counselling. It is useless.'

Let us compare this Maududian dictum with the unbroken tradition of God's messengers. When Noah's[as] people accused him of spreading 'manifest error', he replied:

> O my people, there is no error in me, but I am a Messenger from the Lord
> of the world. I deliver to you the message of my Lord and give you sincere
> advice, and I know from Allah what you do not know. (7.62-3)

This is God's account of Noah's[as] ministry. According to the Maududian dictum, Noah[as] *should* have said: 'I am the Messenger of God and I shall impose upon you, whether you like it or not, a body of righteous men who will take away your power.'

When the people of Ad told Hud[as] he was lost in foolishness, he did not say: 'Do not be deceived and consider me a fool because of the harmlessness of the advice; you are not seeing the real me. In fact, I am an oppressor and one day I will seize power from the hands of those who have rebelled against God and give it to my own, righteous, people.' Indeed, he did not. Instead, he followed the tradition of the prophets and said:

> O my people, there is no foolishness in me, but I am a Messenger from
> the Lord of the worlds. I deliver to you the messages of my Lord and I am
> to you a sincere and faithful counsellor. (7.68-9)

The people of Thamud, like those of Ad, rejected Saleh[as] and accused him of all sorts of things. But, following Noah[as] and Hud[as], he told them: 'O my people, I did deliver the message of my Lord unto you and offered you sincere counsel, but you love not sincere counsellors.' (7.80)

And then God sent Lot[as], whose followers also made no attempt to seize power from the misguided, and continued to reason with them till they were punished. Before the appointed punishment came, Lot[as] and his followers left their homes with God's permission. And then came that morning about which tyrants have always been admonished: 'Hopeless will that morning be for those who have been warned.' (37.178)

The seventh chapter of the Quran continues with the story of the misguided people and the messengers[as] of God who tried to reform them. After telling the story of Lot[as], the Quran tells us how Shuaib[as] reasoned with his arrogant people and pleaded with his cruel tormentors. When all his advice was rejected, he turned away from them and said: 'O my people. indeed, I deliver to you the messages of my Lord and give you sincere counsel. How, then, should I sorrow for a disbelieving people?' (7.94)

The Quran, which for Maulana Maududi and all Muslims is the Word of God, tells us that all God's messengers give sermons and advice and when these are rejected, they cry and pray before their Lord. They have an unshakeable belief in their message and, instead of seizing power from their enemies, they continue to offer love and kindness. They reason gently, impart advice with humility and leave the result to God. He alone is the Lord and He bestows the earth on whoever He pleases. The wishes of all His messengers are epitomised in Moses'[as] words: 'O Lord, send down on us steadfastness and make us die as men who have surrendered to Thee.' (7.127) Moses[as] advised his people, 'to seek help from Allah and wait in patience and constancy' (7.129) and told them that the 'Earth belongs to Allah; He gives it as a heritage to whoever He pleases'. (7.129) It is not for righteous men to seize power by force. All that we know is that 'the end is best for the God-fearing'. (7.129)

After Moses[as], Jesus[as], too, spent his life exhorting and counselling and never considered seizing power. Finally, the chief of all prophets, Muhammad[sa] was sent as an exhorter and counsellor to invite the poeple to be virtuous, not as a kind of a policeman or a soldier. God named him 'admonisher' and said: 'Remind them, for thou art an admonisher. Thou hast no authority to compel them.' (88.22-3)

But the Maulana insists that he and his followers 'are not a body of religious preachers and evangelists, but an organisation of God's troopers so that they "may be a witness against mankind"'. (2.144) The task of these 'troopers' is to use force to wipe out 'injustice, mischief, disorder, disobedience and exploitation from the world'.[14]

God tells the greatest of his prophets: 'We have not appointed thee a keeper over them, nor art thou over them a guardian'. (6.108) But Maulana Maududi reserves for himself and his followers not only the authority of a policeman, but also the powers of a magistrate. It is surprising that God did not give the Prophet[sa], His greatest reformer, temporal authority over the hearts of unbelievers, but gave it instead to Maulana Maududi and his followers. The Holy Prophet[sa] - the embodiment of mercy and compassion - prayed hard that he should become instrumental in showing the path of righteousness to all mankind. But God answered: 'Will thou, then, take it upon thyself to force people to become believers?' (10.100) As far as believers are concerned, God told the Holy Prophet[sa]: 'And if Allah had enforced His will, they would not have set up gods with Him. And We have not made thee as keeper over them, nor art thou over them a guardian.' (6.108)

In contrast to the established conduct of all the messengers of God mentioned in the Holy Quran by name or in general, Maulana Maududi gave himself the authority to oppress and compel God's servants so that the Jamaati Islami could eradicate injustice, mischief, disorders, disobedience and exploitation from the world'.[15]

The Maulana's ambition of seizing power knew no bounds: he would go to any lengths to achieve it. He was totally obsessed with political authority and considered that the worship of God had been prescribed to train Muslims to usurp power and rule the world. For him, worship had no spiritual purpose. It was not a religious experience, a meeting ground between man and his Creator, but a ritual of self-discipline. God says: 'I have created *Jinn* and men that they may worship Me.' (51.57) The world was created for the worship of God. Worship was not created for any other purpose. But the Maulana insists:

> The prayers *(salat)*, fasting, charity *(zakat)* and pilgrimage have been prescribed to prepare and train us for this purpose *(jihad)*. All the governments in the world give their armies special and specific training, their police and civil service too. In the same way, Islam also trains those who join its service - then requires them to go to *jihad* and establish the government of God.[16]

No religion in the world preaches such a materialistic concept of worship. But even the worship of God can become nothing more than an army drill for a person who is obsessed.

Ambition is impatient by definition, but of all ambitions power mania brooks least delay. So the Maulana would not take the straight path - it was too narrow and too long for him. And Marxism, too, will not take the long and hard route of democracy to liberate the oppressed. Instead, it adopts violence to try to overthrow the elected government of the day. The Maulana's method of reform is no different from the Marxist ideology of violent struggle. The Maulana says: 'Stand up to reform people wherever you can. Try to replace wrong principles with correct ones. Snatch away executive and legislative powers from those who do not fear God.[17]

It is surprising that a journalist of Maulana Maududi's long political experience could not understand the principle that governments should not be overthrown by force, whatever the reason. To break this basic rule is to destroy law and order. The fires of civil war would consume the very fabric of society.

Firstly, no party can be its own judge and decide its intentions are good. Secondly, even if those intentions are good, the opposition parties cannot be condemned out of hand. It is inconceivable that every member of the opposition is cruel, unjust or evil, while every member of God's troopers' is pious, God-fearing and free from greed and lust. The fact is that parties which start the work of reform with high-flying claims are the ones which soon become greedy for power, their good intentions burned up by the flames of greed. The Maulana himself explains how uncontrollable is the desire for power:

> As everyone knows, power is such a dangerous demon that the very desire of it is accompanied by an all-consuming greed. Man eagerly looks forward to owning earthly treasures and controlling his fellow creatures so that he may exercise absolute power over them.[18]

One problem in uttering such uncontrolled rhetoric is that even an experienced journalist like Maududi forgets the inherent contradictions within his writings. If the very thought of power can bring a dangerous change of heart, what guarantee is there that the 'upright' members of the Jamaati Islami would not be corrupted by absolute power? No doubt these 'upright' men have undergone the 'civil service training' prescribed by God, i.e. Islamic worship (prayers, fasting and *zakat*), but this 'service training' is not restricted to the Jamaati Islami. Ahmadi worship is not accepted as Islamic worship, according to Maulana Maududi, but what about Brelvi and Deobandi worship? Is Shiite worship not Islamic worship? Would anyone say that the prayers offered by Ahli Quran are non-Islamic? If so, why should not these Muslim sects 'rise against governments based on *false* principles, seize power, remove the *wrongdoers* and establish a government based on *sound* and *just* administration?' 'false', 'wrongdoers', 'sound' and 'just' are relative terms. What is false according to the Jamaati Islami may not be false according to the Deobandis. What is sound and just according to the Deobandis may not be sound and just for the Brelvis. Then, what about non-Muslims? They, too, have their own views about what is right and wrong. If their views were no different from those of Muslims, they would have queued to join Islam. Would they also have had a right to overthrow the government of the day?

Good intentions or reform projects cannot become an excuse to overthrow governments. There are such vast differences in the definition of 'uprightness' between different political parties that if all these differences were accepted, no party could be considered 'upright'. For instance, according to the Maulana, the Ahmadiyyah Movement has no connection with Islam; the British government created it to divide the Muslim *umma* so that Muslims would be dissuaded from *jihad* and their strength sapped. It is alleged that the movement was developed to act as a fifth column to destroy the Muslim *umma* from within.

But the Ahmadi self-image is very different from that of the Jamaati Islami. Ahmadis believe their movement was founded to establish supremacy and to bring about a Muslim rebirth. It was not the British, but God Himself, who planted its seed to fulfil a promise He made to the people of Muhammad[sa]. He promised to send a Mahdi for the reform of the *umma* and raise a Messiah who, with his irrefutable reasoning, would destroy the Cross, the Cross which inflicted suffering on Jesus[as]. It is that Mahdi and that Messiah who founded this community, now busy in the selfless service of mankind. On one hand, the community humbly counsels and advises people to change themselves, while, on the other, it fights and defeats Christianity on every front. How can one believe that the Ahmadiyyah Movement was set up by the British - themselves Christian? Does one expect the British to support, let alone found, a community which is devoted to eradicating the Trinity and planting the holy tree of the Unity of God? Wherever Ahmadis have gone, the weed of the Trinity has withered and the ever-beautiful plant of the Unity has flourished with fragrant flowers and sweet fruits. If that is the fruit of a plant sown by the British, then one only wishes they had sown a few more, so that the revival of Islam and the dissolution of Christianity had been accelerated!

What Ahmadis believe about themselves is exactly the opposite of the Maulana's views about them. In the Ahmadiyyah view, the founder of their movement was deeply immersed in the love of the Holy Prophet, Muhammad[sa]. The following lines from one of his poems show the ecstasy of his love and the depth of his devotion for the Holy Prophet[sa]:

> My intoxication in the loving of Muhammad[sa] is second only to that of God
>
> If this can be dubbed as disbelief, then God be my witness that I am the greatest of disbelievers.   *Durre Thameen*

According to the Ahmadis, their belief is deeply rooted in the love of the Seal of the Prophet, Muhammad[sa]. But Maulana Maududi asserts that their roots go deep into the British soil of imperialism. The two views are entirely opposed.

Let us examine the converse view. The Maulana asserts that the Jamaati Islami has been founded to create a body of 'upright' men through a long discipline of Islamic worship. These people should reach such a point of readiness that Islam can say to them: 'Yes, now you are the most upright servants of God on earth. Forward, Muslim soldiers, fight the rebels of God, dispossess them of authority and take the reins of government in your hands.' Thanks to the Maulana's efforts, that body of upright men is now ready and waiting to gain strength to overthrow the government of the day.

The Maulana really believes that this body of 'upright' men was created to reform mankind and raise Islam's flag in the world. It will abolish everything ungodly and carve with the sword the name of Allah on every heart.

The Maulana's claim that the members of Jamaati Islami are the most upright servants of God is believed to be baseless by the Ahmadis. As a matter of principle, everyone has the right to consider himself and his followers to be in the right. To be right is one thing. To be upright is quite another. We cannot claim we are righteous and upright. Man is lost in a maze of self-deception, delusion and outright hypocrisy, so that he is unable to describe himself with any accuracy. Who knows the secrets of the heart, the lust of the mind and the hidden desires, except God? Only He knows who is upright and who sins. There are exceptions, of course. Some people exhibit unmistakeable and conclusive signs of their up-rightness, so that the love of God is evident from their behaviour. God talks with them as He talked with the upright people of the past. His light shines over them as it did over the great mystics and saints of the *umma* and His succour and support becomes manifest, both in words and deeds.

Therefore Ahmadis totally reject Maulana Maududi's claim that the Jamaati Islami was founded to raise the flag of Islam. That is, in fact, a degrading and defaming of the religion which he professes to follow. The followers of Maulana Maududi can claim whatever they want within the safety of a Muslim country like Pakistan or Saudi Arabia, but let them take their creed of 'Islam by force' elsewhere and just see what reception it gets. Can they convert Christians, with their belief in Jesus[as] living since his crucifixion in heaven, to Islam? Can they destroy the Cross? Can anyone raise the flag of Islam with these Maududian beliefs?

There is no doubt in an Ahmadi mind that the teaching of Maulana Maududi brings Islam into disrepute and makes it a target of ridicule. The Jamaati Islami is not only not a friend of Islam, but also it is a form of communism. Devoid of spiritual values, hungry for power, the Jamaati Islami is inspired by Moscow, not Mecca.

In short, Ahmadis censure the Jamaati Islami as greatly as the Maulana censures the Ahmadiyyah for supposedly being abusive and vituperative. Multiply these two opposing views among other sects and groups of the *umma* and you will see each of them tearing apart the other's claim of uprightness. Who, then, should 'Stand up to reform people and snatch away the executive and legislative powers from people who have no fear of God?'

Power obsession is the focal point of Maulana Maududi's concept of reform. He sees the Prophet's[sa] life in political terms, explains Islamic worship in military jargon and interprets the Quran as pure power politics. The Maulana knows he is incapable of reforming by persuasion, patience and humility, so he puts forward a policy of violence and disorder. The most generous interpretation of his aims is that his intentions were good. But the road to hell is paved with good intentions. The Quranic verdict, however, is explicit: 'When it is said to them: Create not disorder in the land, they retort: We are only seeking to promote peace. Take note - most certainly it is they who create disorder, but they realise it not. (2.12-13)

CHAPTER 5

THE MAUDUDIAN LAW OF APOSTASY

Surely, this is a reminder; so whoever wishes may take the way that leads to his Lord.

Quran, 76.30

In our domain we neither allow any Muslim to change his religion nor allow any other religion to propagate its faith.

Maulana Maududi[1]

Maulana Maududi's desire for political power knew no bounds. The law of apostasy which he evolved was an extension of his dictatorial and intolerant personality - it had nothing to do with Islam. Dr Israr Ahmad, who worked closely with Maududi, said that Maududi borrowed the principles of his movement from Maulana Abul Kalam Azad and the Khairi brothers and the style of his presentation from Niyaz Fatehpuri. But he was so egocentric that he never acknowledged that his ideas came from anyone but himself.[2]

Similarly, the Maulana's ideas on apostasy, though originating from an interpretive error of early Muslim jurisprudence (*fiqh*) are, in fact, based on medieval Christianity. The Deoband school,[3] which was on one hand collaborating with a predominantly Hindu political organisation - the Indian National Congress - and on the other fighting a rearguard action against the *shuddi* campaign, provided the gloss to Maududi's thoughts on the subject. The influence of Marxist writings, which the Maulana seems to have read when a young and impressionable editor, is markedly noticeable in his thinking. The *Tahrik-i Jamaati Islami* is a curious blend of medieval Christian practices, Deobandi/Wahabi intolerance and Marxist incitement to disruption.

As we saw in the first chapter of this book, the concept of religious

49

liberty is not evolutionary or lineal - it is a cyclical phenomenon. Whenever one of God's prophets or a religious reformer appears, he is opposed. He is accused of dividing the community and breaking traditional conformity. He is pilloried as an apostate. Ultimately a prophet always succeeds in establishing religious freedom. The true faith spread by this religious freedom is hardened in rigid dogma, which actually results in the loss of the right to dissent.

On his last visit to the Temple, Christ[as] said: 'Render unto Caesar the things that are Caesar's, and unto God the things that are God's.' (Mark 12:17) This very clear statement separates religious belief from political authority. However, within a year of obtaining political authority (312), the Christian Church was torn by schism. For more than 300 years Christians had been persecuted and flourished, and yet, soon after Constantine's conversion, the Church was confronted with monastic secession, Donatist schism and Arian heresy. Throughout the history of the Christian Church, heresy, or deviation from orthodoxy, has been a matter of deep concern. It invariably involves the very concept of deity, the divinity of Christ[as].

> If Christ was divine in an absolute sense, yet distinct from God, there were two Gods and Christianity was a form of ditheism, not monotheism. On the other hand, if the filial relationship were literally interpreted, then God the Father would be the progenitor of God the Son. But the logic of this relationship meant that Christ would not be fully God, since there must have been a time when he 'was not' and God the Father alone existed.[4]

Orthodox Christians held Christ[as] to be identical in being (homousinous) to God the Father, while Arius (c. 256-336) considered him only similar in being (homoiousios) to Him. Then there was the question of his mother. Nestorious (died c. 451) declared that Jesus[as] was two distinct persons, one human, one divine; and that Mary[as] was the mother only of the human, not the divine Christ[as]. It would be better, therefore, to call her the mother of Christ[as]. The orthodox doctrine is that Mary[as] is the true mother, not of the Godhead itself, but of the incarnate *legos*, or Word of God, containing both the divine and the human natures of Christ[as].[5]

The first ecumenical Council of the Church met in 325 in Bithynian Nicea and issued a creed on the mystery of the Trinity. The unrepentant Arius was anathamatised by the council and exiled by Emperor Constantine. The emperor also ordered that all Arius's books should be burned and their possession should be punished by death.

The cycle of religious liberty which began with Jesus of Nazareth[as] came full circle when Justinian (483-565) prescribed the death penalty for apostasy. The penalty became part of the codification of Roman law in AD535.

It is a tragic twist of fate that freedom of conscience was snuffed out by the very Roman Christians whose newly converted forefathers were burned to provide fire and fun in Nero's Rome (AD64). As long as Christians were persecuted by non-Christian political authorities, Christian writers defended religious liberty. But once the imperial throne was won over to Christianity, the Church looked 'with the same hostile eye upon individualism in belief as the state upon secession or revolt'.[6] By the middle of the fifth century things that were and still are God's were rendered unto Caesar. Political authority had become the right arm of the Church. In the course of his campaign against the Donatists, St Augustine (354-430) argued: 'There is a righteous persecution which the Church of Christ inflicts upon the impious. She persecutes in the spirit of love . . . that she may correct . . . that she may recall from error . . . [taking] measures for their good, to secure their eternal salvation.'[7]

In 385 a Spanish bishop, Priscillian, was accused of preaching Manicheism and universal celibacy. He denied the charge, but was tried, condemned and burned at the stake with several companions.

Martin Luther (1483-1546), the German leader of the Protestant Reformation, concurred with his Roman Catholic predecessor, Augustine, and said: 'The clergy had authority over conscience, but it was thought necessary that they should be supported by the State with absolute penalties of outlawry, in order that error might be exterminated, although it was impossible to banish sin.'[8]

But it was the French Protestant theologican John Calvin (1509-64) who really inspired Maulana Maududi.

> He [Calvin] wished to extend religion by the sword and reserve death as the punishment of apostasy. . . . Catholics should suffer the same penalties as those who were guilty of sedition, on the grounds that the majesty of God must be as strictly avenged as the throne of the king.[9]

While the inspiration came to the Maulana from Calvin, the rationale was provided by the English thinker Thomas Hobbes (1588-1679) in his book, *Leviathan*. Since the power to work miracles is one of the signs of a true prophet, and, according to Hobbes, the days of miracles were over, there was no possibility of guidance by a prophet or through divine inspiration. The sovereign alone had civil or religious authority. He alone had the power to make law, 'For whosoever hath a lawful power over any writing, to make it law, hath the power also to approve or disapprove the interpretation of the same.'[10]

Heresy, in Hobbes's view, was private judgement and action contrary to popular belief as laid down by the sovereign:

> It is not the intrinsic error of the judgment that makes the heresy punishable, but the private rebellion against authority. To make loyalty to the commands of conscience the ruling principle would sanction all private men to disobey their princes in maintenance of their religion, true or false.[11]

According to Hobbes, this is subversion.

There is no apostasy without heresy and no heresy without dogma. The Roman Catholic dogma was carefully spelled out in the Athanasian Creed, which says: 'That we worship one God in Trinity, and Trinity in Unity; Neither confounding the Persons: nor dividing the Substance.'

It is in this tradition of medieval Christianity, and not of Islam, that Maulana Maududi developed the original ideals of Maulana Abul Kalam Azad and the Khairi brothers' *Hukumat-i-Ilahiyya* (*Kingdom of God*).[12] St Augustine, Martin Luther, John Calvin and Thomas Hobbes provided him with the non-Islamic concepts of orthodoxy, dogma and heresy - and also with the rhetoric of intolerance.

Even the orientalists, who never miss an opportunity of criticising Islam, agree there is no dogma and heresy in Islam. Goldziher says:

> The role of dogma in Islam cannot be compared to that which it plays in religious life of any of the Christian Churches. There are no Councils and Synods which, after lively controversy, lay down the formulae, which henceforth shall be deemed to embrace the whole of the true faith. There is no ecclesiastical institution, which serves as the measure of orthodoxy; no single authorised interpretation of the holy scriptures, on which the doctrine and exegesis of the church might be built. The Consensus, the supreme authority in all questions of religious practice, exercises an elastic, in a certain sense barely definable jurisdiction, the very conception of which is moreover variously explained. Particularly in unanimity what shall have effect as undisputed Consensus. What is accepted as Consensus by one party, is far from being accepted as such by another.[13]

The contemporary Jewish orientalist, Bernard Lewis, who would never be accused of being pro-Muslim, observes:

> What matters was what people did - orthopraxy, rather than orthodoxy - and Muslims were allowed on the whole to believe as they chose to do, so long as they accepted the basic minimum, the Unity of God and the apostolate of Muhammad, and conformed to the social norms.[14]

True Islam had ceased to be the inspiring force for Maulana Maududi.

Having introduced the concepts of heresy and apostasy he could not escape from Calvin's logic which prescribed 'death as the punishment of apostasy'. But the Maulana had the audacity falsely to attribute the authority for this punishment to the Holy Prophet[sa]. The Maulana wrote a pamphlet on the subject in which he confidently quoted Abu Bakr's military action against the rebel tribes as a proof that there was a death penalty for apostasy. Before discussing this, one ought to quote the Maulana's writings to show how heavily he was influenced by his Christian models.

But first, in summary, to the Christian fathers of medieval Europe, recantation from Christianity was punishable by death and the only acceptable definition of Christianity was theirs. Similarly, the punishment for recantation from Islam was death and the only definition of Islam was the one the Maulana or his successors laid down. It is clear that under a Maududian government, the Maududian ruler would decide who was and who was not a Muslim. What would that decision be? The Maulana's writings are quite clear.

According to Maududi, Ahmadis are apostates and a 'non-Muslim minority'. But Ahmadis are not the only heretics - the Ahl-i-Quran, the followers of Mr Parvez's school of thought, are also heretics. They are *kafir* and apostates. In fact, their heresy is far more serious than that of the Qadiyanis. The following order of banishment given by Maulana Amin Ahsan Islahi, who had not yet renounced the Maududian teaching - and was still considered the right-hand man of Maududi - was published in the *Tasnim*, the official organ of the Jamaati Islami:

> Some people advise that since there is no possibility of the promulgation of the Islamic Sharia, the government of this country [Pakistan] should be formed on the principles laid down in the Quran. If, by this, these people mean that the Sharia is confined *only* to the Quran and that other rules are not Sharia, then it is clearly heresy. This heresy is similar to that of the Qadiyanis, in fact, much more serious.[15]

This verdict is clearly against the Ahmadis and the Ahl-i-Quran. To discover whether 'heresy' and consequent apostasy is confined to only these two groups needs a closer look.

According to Maulana Maududi's writings, anything *not* Maududian is heresy. The Maududian teachings are like the Athanasian Creed and any deviation from them is *kufr*. The Maulana says:

> Ninety-nine point nine per cent of the Muslim nation has no knowledge of Islam or the ability to tell right from wrong. They have directed neither their moral values nor their thoughts towards Islam. A Muslim is a

Muslim because his father was a Muslim and the faith is passed from generation to generation. These Muslims have not accepted this right because they believe it to be right, and neither have they rejected the wrong because they know it to be wrong. If Muslim affairs are ever handed over to these people and anyone thinks Muslim affairs will be properly run, he's living in fool's paradise.[16]

He continues:

The process of democratic elections is like churning milk to obtain butter. If poisoned milk is churned, the butter will be poisonous too. So people who think that the Kingdom of God [Hukumat-i-Ilahiyya] will automatically result if Muslim areas are liberated from the Hindu majority, are wrong. They will end up with a heretic government of Muslims [Kafirana hukumat].[17]

The Maulana is more explicit in the following passage of the same book:

The nation called Musulman is made up of all kinds of rubbish. All types of characters found among unbelievers are found here. The number of liars appearing in law courts is no less than in the courts of other nations. Bribery, theft, adultery, falsehood, in short, there is no form of moral depravity in which they are second to the unbelievers. [kuffar].[18]

These Maududian edicts and injunctions are very comprehensive. However, some may still doubt that these injunctions refer to the ordinary 99.99 per cent of Muslims and that Muslim leadership and intellectuals are exempt from these constraints. But the Maulana made another statement about Muslim leaders and *ulema* to make it clear that any Muslim who does not accept the Maududian creed has gone astray. The Maulana says:

Western educated political leaders, *ulema*, and the scholars of Muslim jurisprudence, all these leaders are as misguided as each other, both in their means and their ends. They have lost the path of truth and have wandered blindly into the darkness. Not one of them has a Muslim point of view.[19]

So, according to the Maulana, neither the 99.99 per cent of Muslims nor their religious or secular leaders are on the right path. They have gone astray, their point of view is not Muslim, and all types of criminals found among the *kuffar* are also found among Muslims. If one were to have dubbed the *umma* a 'bunch of apostates' on hearing this description, Maududi would have replied: 'You said it.' He was not in the habit of mincing his words. Referring to those who quit the Jamaati Islami, he said: 'This is not the path on which to retreat. To retreat means to apostasise.'[20] If quitting the Jamaati Islami and joining another Muslim group is apostasy, then that other organisation is automatically *kafir*. So are Muslims who pray for favours at saints' tombs and also the Shiites, who consider the first three caliphs to be usurpers. It is well known that according to the Maulana - and all the *ulema* of Deoband agree with him - the mainstream *Ahli Sunnat wal Jamaat* of India and Pakistan, known as Brelvis, are *kafir*.

Now that the Maulana has, virtually declared all non-Maududians to be apostates, he deals in great detail with the subject of people who are Muslim by birth. It is one of the most difficult pieces of Maududi's argument. Discussing his own Islam, the Maulana said: 'I have cast away the collar of inherited Islam . . . . I read the Quran and studied the life of Muhammad[sa] . . . and now I am a new (converted) Muslim.' On the same basis, he devised a scheme for the reconversion of other Muslims. He unveils his plan in the following words:

> Whenever the death penalty for apostasy is enforced in a new Islamic state, then Muslims are kept within Islam's fold. But there is a danger that a large number of hypocrites will live alongside them. They will always pose a danger of treason.
>
> My solution to the problem is this. That whenever an Islamic revolution takes place, all non-practising Muslims should, within one year, declare their turning away from Islam and get out of Muslim society. After one year all born Muslims will be considered Muslim. All Islamic laws will be enforced upon them. They will be forced to practice all the *fara id and wajibat* of their religion and, if anyone then wishes to leave Islam, he will be executed. Every effort will be made to save as many people as possible from falling into the lap of *kufr*. But those who cannot be saved will be reluctantly separated from society forever [executed]. After this purification Islamic society will start afresh with Muslims who have decided voluntarily to remain Muslims.[21]

The Maulana does not tell us under what rules of *ijtihad* a law laying down the death penalty for apostasy will be relaxed. In any case this law will be relaxed only at the time an Islamic state is established - a one-off concession. After this period of grace, Muslims who are born *kafirs* will lose out. The Maulana explains why he is unable to make any exception for these unfortunates. He says:

> There is one final question about capital punishment which may distrub many of us. A non-Muslim who freely embraced Islam then returned to *kufr* can be said to have made a deliberate mistake. He could have remained a *dhimmi*, so why enter a religion of collective responsibility from which there is no escape? But what of the person who was born of Muslim parents and who has not embraced Islam? He is a Muslim by birth. If, on reaching adulthood, he wants to reject the faith, you threaten

him with execution and he remains Muslim. This is unjust. And it also provides sustenance to the ever-growing number of born hypocrites in Muslim society. There are two answers to this question, one deals with the practical aspect, the other with the principle. In principle there can be no distinction between the born followers of a religion and that religion's converts. And no religion has ever made that distinction. Both converts and born followers are governed by the same laws. It is both impossible and a logical absurdity to treat the children of the followers of a religion as *kufar* or aliens till they are adults, then give them the choice of choosing or rejecting the religion (or citizenship, for that matter) of their birth. No society in the world could manage its affairs in this way.[22]

Even if we accept the Maududian law that Islam prescribes death for apostasy and that all Muslims except Jamaati Islami are *kafir*, we cannot treat non-Maududian Muslims as apostates - even according to the Maulana's own logic. They are 'born *kafir*'. The Maulana wants to have his cake and eat it too! Muslims who disagree with the Maududian concept of Islam are first described as both 'born Muslims' and *kafir*, because they were brought up by their parents in a *kafirana* environment. Then they are called apostates because on reaching the age of consent they did not reject their parents' Islam in preference to Maududian Islam. A non-Muslim who joins Islam and then recants should be executed because he became Muslim knowing full well there was no escape. Similarly, a non-Maududian-born Muslim should also be treated as an apostate because he did not accept Maulana Maududi's version of Islam on reaching adulthood. This is the argument which clearly shows the Maulana's dictatorial, manipulative and intolerant personality. No Muslim, convert or born, is out of his reach. The Quranic ordinance that 'there shall be no compulsion in religion' is explained away in the following words:

> This means we do not compel anyone to embrace our religion. This is true. But we must warn anyone who wishes to recant that this door is impassable to free traffic. If you wish to come, do so with the firm decision that you cannot escape.

A leading scholar of the Ahl-i Quran, Ghulam Ahmad Parvez, referring to this Maududian commentary on the Quranic verse, said 'Maududi Sahib's Islam is a mouse-trap: the mouse can get into it, but cannot escape.'

The central point of the Maulana's argument is that every religion considers the descendants of its followers as its followers. Therefore, descendants of Muslim parents - even where the parents are practically *kafir* - will be Islamic property. If a right of ownership has been established over these children, how can they be free to choose another religion on reaching adulthood? In explaining this point, the Maulana seems to have overlooked the following saying of the Prophet[sa] 'Every infant has an in-born predisposition to be a Muslim, but his parents make him a Jew or a Christian or a Zoroastrian.[23] If the central point of the Maulana's argument is correct, then why confine it to the descendants of Muslims? Why not apply it to those of non-Muslims too, since they, according to the *hadith*, were also born with a 'predisposition to be Muslim'? This would give full control of every non-Muslim child to the Maududian government. It makes no difference whether a child is within the Maududian realm or not. While the Maulana seems to have over-looked that *hadith* quoted above, the force of his logic leads him to this absurdity.

Maulana Maududi has, in fact, reproduced medieval Christianity almost word for word in the Jamaati Islami movement. Commenting on his policy of intolerance, Elisabeth Labrousse, an historian of medieval Christianity, observes: 'On the individual level, it creates only martyrs or hypocrites.'[24] Now compare Labrousse's observation with the following passage from Maududi's *The Punishment of Apostasy in Islam*: 'If he [the apostate] is really so honest in not wishing to live as a hypocrite and really does wish to remain steadfast in his own faith, why does he not present himself for death?'[25]

Since the Maududian concept of religion is the only way to salvation, the Maulana would not allow the same rights and privileges to the followers of any other religion. The missionary work of other religions would be forbidden in a Maududian state. The Maulana says:

> The execution of apostates has already decided the issue. Since we do not allow any Muslim to embrace any other religion, the question of allowing other religions to open their missions and propagate their faiths within our boundaries does not arise. We cannot tolerate it.[26]

But can a *kafir* propagate his religion among other *kafirs*? For instance, can a Christian open missions to work among Jews or Hindus? Could Arya Samajists, who do not believe in idol worship and believe in one God, preach to the followers of pantheist Sanatan Dharma? The Maulana says:

> Islam can never tolerate that false religions should spread in the world. How can the missionaries of false religions be given a licence to spread falsehood and attract others to the fire towards which they themselves are advancing?[27]

Maududi himself accepts that Jews and Christians are Ahl-i Kitab (people of the Book). But if they wish to convert idol worshippers, fire worshippers or polytheists to the worship of one God - the God of Moses[as] and Jesus[as] - thus bringing them nearer to Islam, they would be forbidden.

In short, the Maulana concedes only that a born *kafir* cannot be killed if he does not accept Islam. But if this is so, why kill a new *kafir* who has recanted? If a new *kafir* is to be punished at all, why the death penalty? Why not exile, or life imprisonment, so that Muslim society may not be disrupted? Here Maulana Maududi, true to St Augustinian logic, explains that the apostate is executed in his own interests. He says:

> There are only two methods of dealing with an apostate. Either make him an outlaw by depriving him of his citizenship and allowing him mere existence, or end his life. The first method is definitely more severe than the second, because he exists in a state in which 'he neither lives nor dies'.[28] Killing him is preferable. That way both his agony and the agony of society are ended simultaneously.[29]

But the punishment to which the Maulana is sentencing apostates is not actually St Augustine's 'spirit of love' persecution. There is a life after death and by killing an apostate, the Maulana is directly consigning him to the fires of hell. By saving an apostate from the temporary agonies of an outcast's life, the Maulana is sending him to the far greater agonies of hell. Above all, the Maulana is depriving the tragic apostate of the opportunity of repentance and therefore salvation. While a *kafir* has the opportunity of repenting at any stage in his life, the apostate cannot return to Islam and benefit from the compassion of the Great Forgiver (*Al-Ghaffar*) and the Acceptor of Repentance (*Al-Tawwab*).

Reducing the Maulana's logic to its absurd conclusion, one might as well ask: 'Since the death penalty is meant to discourage people who take change of faith lightly from entering our society, how do you propose to stop such wavering people from being born into Muslim homes?'

This Draconian policy of force and brutal intolerance is not restricted to the Maududian state. Its foreign policy is also based on force and intolerance. The Maulana says:

> Islam does not want to bring about this revolution in one country or a few countries. It wants to spread it to the entire world. Although it is the duty of the 'Muslim Party' to bring this revolution first to its own nation, its ultimate goal is world revolution.

Of course, the final goal of Islam is world revolution. But Islam wants a *spiritual* revolution, not the communist revolution which the Maulana has borrowed from communist ideology. It is no accident that Maududian polemic closely follow communist argument. Substitute the words 'Communist Party' and you find the echoes of Marx and Lenin in Maulana Maududi's writings. The Maududian revolution is not based on *adl* (justice) but on materialism and consequent personal dictatorship. Maududian policy towards neighbouring states and communist foreign policy are not very much different.

Maulana Maududi writes:

Human relations are so integrated that no state can have complete freedom of action under its principles unless the same principles are not in force in a neighbouring country. Therefore, a 'Muslim Party' will not be content with the establishment of Islam in just one area alone - both for its own safety and the general reform. It should try to expand in all directions. On one hand it will spread its ideology, on the other it will invite people of all nations to accept its creed, for salvation lies only therein. *If this Islamic state has power and resources it will fight and destroy non-Islamic governments and establish Islamic states in their place.*[30]

The paragraph above is virtually a *mutatis mutandis* copy of the Communist Manifesto.

The Maulana has no hesitation in attributing his aggressive policy to the Holy Prophet[sa] himself. He says:

This was the policy adopted by the Prophet[sa] and his rightly guided caliphs. Arabia, where the Muslim Party was first formed, was the first to be subdued. After this the Prophet[sa] sent invitations to all neighbouring countries. *But he did not wait to see whether they were accepted or not.* As soon as he acquired power, he started the conflict with the Roman Empire. Abu Bakr became the leader of the party after the Prophet[sa] and attacked both the Roman and Persian Empires, while Umar finally won the war.[31]

This is a general declaration of war against all non-Muslim neighbouring states - they are safe only as long as the Maududian state is weak. As soon as the Maududian state has given one year's notice to its Muslim-born subjects to opt for Maududian Islam or get out and has subdued domestic opposition, it will engage in a war of conquest against its neighbours. Maududi does not agree with the generally held Muslim view that war was actually forced upon the Prophet[sa], Abu Bakr and Umar by powerful Christian and Zoroastrian empires wishing to crush Islam, and that Muslims, despite having fewer resources, had to fight back in self-defence.

CHAPTER 6

RECANTATION UNDER ISLAM

Write down for me the name of everyone who calls himself a Muslim.
Muhammad[sa]

The concept of apostasy, as it existed in medieval Christianity and as expounded by Maulana Maududi, is alien to Islam. There is not even a word for it in the Arabic language. There is no doubt that some early Muslim scholars of law (*fiqh*) considered recantation from Islam to be a capital offence, but their definition of 'Muslim' was so broad that no one calling himself a Muslim could be called a recanter. The Prophet[sa] gave us two definitions of a Muslim. At the time of the first census of Medina, the Prophet[sa] said: 'Write down for me the name of everyone who calls himself a Muslim.'[1] On another occasion the Prophet[sa] said: 'Whoever prays as we pray and turns to our *Qiblah* and eats what we ritually slaughter is a Muslim; he is *dhimmat-Allah* and *dhimmat al-rasul*. So do not put Allah in contravention of his *dhimmah* [responsibility].'[2]

But Maulana Maududi and the *ulema*, supporting dictatorships and autocracies in Muslim countries, have added various qualifications to the Prophet's[sa] simple definition. In the words of Al-Ghazali (450-505AH/ AD1058-1113) they have limited: 'The vast Mercy of God to make paradise the preserve of a small clique of theologians.'[3] The result of their effort has been summed up by the former chief justice of Pakistan, Muhammad Munir, who presided over the Court of Inquiry into the Punjab (Pakistan) Disturbances in 1953. He said:

> Keeping in view the several definitions given by the *ulema*, need we make any comment except that no two learned divines are agreed on this fundamental? If we attempt our own definition, as each learned divine has, and that definition differs from all others, we all leave Islam's fold. If we adopt the definition given by any one of the *ulema*, we remain Muslims according to the view of that *alim*, but *kafirs* according to everyone else's definition.[4]

Justice Munir's observation must be read with reference to the Prophet'sˢᵃ reprimand to Usama b. Zayd. In the raid of Ghalib b. Abdullah al-Kalbi, according to Ibn Ishaq, a man was killed by Usama b. Zayd and another. Reporting this incident, Usama b. Zayd said:

> When I and a man of Ansar overtook him and attacked him with our weapons he pronounced the *Shahadah*, but we did not stay our hands and killed him. When we came to the Prophetˢᵃ and told him what had happened, he said: 'Who will absolve you, Usama, from ignoring the confession of faith?' I told him that the man had pronounced the words merely to escape death, but he repeated his question and continued to do so until I wished that I had never been a Muslim before that day and that I had never killed the man. I asked him to forgive me and promised that I would never kill a man who pronounced the *Shahadah*. The Prophetˢᵃ said: 'You will say it after me (after my death), Usama?' and I said that I would.[5]

The Prophetˢᵃ knew that despite his concern for the lives of *Shahadah*-pronouncing Muslims, they would still be killed by misguided people under Islam's name. According to the report in the *Musnad Imam Ahmad Hanbal*, the Prophetˢᵃ also asked Osama whether he had opened his victim's heart to check the authenticity of his faith.[6] And yet the power-hungry and politically orientated *ulema* continue to incite ignorant Muslims to kill their Muslim brothers - Muslims whose viewpoint differed slightly from their own - as if, on opening their hearts, they had discovered their faith was false.

Regarding recantation, the Quran uses the word *irtadda*, which means that no one has the right to declare any other Muslim *murtadd*. As Imam Raghib Isfahani[7] explains, the word *irtidad* means to retrace one's steps back to the point from where one came. The word is especially associated with recantation - returning to *kufr* (disbelief) from Islam, e.g. 'Lo! Those who turn their backs after the guidance hath been manifested unto them'; (47.26) and 'whoso of you becometh renegade from his religion'. (5.55)

Ridda is an intransitive verb and its root, *rdd*, has no transitive form; a person can recant, but no one else can make him a recanter. It is a voluntary action and no outside agency can play any part in it. It is this aspect of free will which distinguishes *irtidad* from the Christian and Maududian concept of apostasy, which we discussed in the last chapter. Apostasy and its punishment requires an external authority, the church or state. It is like execution or, rather, murder. *Irtidad* is like suicide. One can execute or murder but no one can 'suicide' someone.

Surah Al-Kafirun, revealed in the early period of the Prophet's[sa] ministry, is a direct statement of policy on the subject of freedom of conscience. The Prophet[sa] was asked to tell unbelievers there was absolutely no meeting-point between their way of life and his. As they were in complete disagreement, not only with regard to the basic concepts of religion, but also with regard to its details and other aspects, there could not possibly be any compromise between them. Hence, 'For you, your religion, for me, my religion'. (109.6)

The Prophet[sa] was also repeatedly told not to worry if unbelievers were not ready to accept his message. He was not their *wakil* (guardian). God says: 'Thy people have rejected the message that We have sent through thee, though it is the truth. Say: "I am not appointed a *wakil* over you."'[8] This statement was made in the Meccan period, when the Prophet[sa] and his followers were persecuted. Yet on his arrival in Medina, the statement was exactly the same, even though he now had power. It was, in fact, made even more explicit.

The first Medinite *surah* in which the subject of freedom of conscience was discussed was *Al-Baqarah*. The 256th verse of the *surah* contains the clearest pronouncement on the subject:

> There shall be no compulsion in religion. Surely guidance has become distinct from error, whosoever refuses to be led by those who transgress and believes in Allah has surely grasped a strong handle which knows no breaking. And Allah is All-Hearing, All-Knowing.

This is the confident declaration of a prophet who has organised an *umma* in a town where his power is supreme. Lest the subject of *jihad* be misunderstood, Muslims are told that true virtue lies in good works and good faith (168-242) and the Majesty of God is called to mind in the Throne verse (255). The commandment of 'no compulsion in religion' comes immediately after the Throne verse. Readers of the Quran might have thought God wanted Muslims to spread Islam by force, because of its call to fight the *umma's* enemies and to offer special sacrifices to Allah. So the verse tells Muslims in no uncertain terms not to resort to violence in the name of conversion. The importance of this verse can be gauged from a *hadith* quoted in *Jami* of *Tirmidhi*. He said that the peak of the Quran is *Al-Baqarah* and that Satan shall not enter the house of anyone who recites ten verses of this chapter (i.e. the first four verses, the Throne verse, the two verses which follow it - 256-257 - and the last three verses).

This principle of no compulsion was reiterated after the victory of

Badr (3.21) and again in *Al-Ma'idah*, which is the last revealed *surah*. Now that Muhammad's[sa] authority was fully established, not only in Medina but also in Mecca, it was vital to emphasise that the Prophet's[sa] only role was to convey the word of Allah. 'Obey Allah and obey the Messenger, and be on your guard, but if you turn away, then remember that the duty of our Messenger is only to convey the message clearly.' (5.93) And finally: 'The Messenger's duty is only to convey the message. *And Allah knows what you reveal and what you hide.*' (5.100) Religious belief is a personal matter. It is God alone - not the state or the religious authorities - who knows what one reveals to God or what one hides.

This verse leads to the subject of *munafiqun* - the hypocrites. The term *munafiqun* describes those inhabitants of Medina who had outwardly accepted Islam, but whose belief was suspect for various reasons. There are many references to them in the Quran, but in four passages they are defined as *murtadd* (recanters). The first reference is in *Surah Muhammad*. This is a Medinite *surah* which briefly describes the aims of war according to Islam. It says that while believers welcome a revelation calling on them to fight for Allah, *munafiqun* feel as if they are being led to their slaughter. In this way, true believers are separated from those whose faith is shallow or false. It goes on to say:

> Surely those who turn their backs [*artaddu*] after guidance has become manifest to them, Satan has seduced them, and holds out false hopes to them. That is because they said to those who hate what Allah has revealed, 'We will obey you in some matters' and Allah knows their secrets. (47:26-27)

The verses quoted above mention no punishment for these people.

The next reference to the *munafiqun* is in the *Surah Al-Munafiqun*, which was revealed towards the end of 6AH/AD628. The *surah* exposes the infidelity and dishonesty of the *munafiqun* and condemns their open profession of faith as false and treacherous. This was a public reprimand:

> Allah bears witness that the *munafiqun* are liars. Their faith is a pretext so that they may turn people away from the way of Allah. Evil is that which they practice. That is because they believed and thereafter disbelieved; so a seal was set upon their hearts and they have no understanding. ... They are the enemy, so beware! ... it is the same for them whether thou ask for forgiveness for them or not. Allah will never forgive them, surely Allah guides not a rebellious people. (63.2-7)

The last two references to the *munafiqun* are in one of the last *surahs*, *Al-Taubah*: 'Offer no excuse, you have certainly disbelieved after having believed. If we forgive a group of you, a group shall we punish, for they have been guilty.' (9.66) Those to be forgiven are obviously *munafiqun* who repented and became sincere Muslims. As regards those who are to be punished, the subsequent verse says: 'Allah promises the *munafiqun* - both men and women - and the disbelievers the fire of hell, wherein they shall abide. It will suffice them. And they shall have everlasting punishment.' (9.68) And, finally:

> They swear by Allah that they said nothing, but they did say the word of disbelief *and did disbelieve after they had embraced Islam*.... So if they repent, it will be better for them, but if they turn away, Allah will punish them with a grievous punishment in this world and the hereafter. And they shall have neither friend nor helper in the earth. (9.74)[9]

The Prophet[sa] knew that Abdullah b. Ubayy b. Salul was the leader of the *munafiqun*, but he took no action against him. On the contrary, the Prophet[sa] prayed for him when he died. Umar b. al-Khattab is reported to have said:

> When the Prophet[sa] went and stood by the dead body of Abdullah b. Ubayy and was about to pray, I asked him: 'Are you going to pray over God's enemy?' The Prophet[sa] smiled and said: 'Get behind me, Umar. I have been given a choice and I have chosen. It was said to me: 'Ask pardon for them or ask it not. If you ask pardon for them seventy times God will not pardon them' If I knew that by asking pardon more than seventy times he would be forgiven, I would do it.' Then he prayed over him and walked with his dead body and stayed at his grave until he was buried.[10]

Freedom of conversion is the acid test of 'no compulsion in religion'. It cannot be a one-way freedom - the freedom to enter Islam, but not to leave it. There are ten direct references to recantation in the Quran: one in the Meccan *surah* of *Al-Nahl* and the remaining nine in the Medinite *surahs*. In none of these verses is there the slightest hint of capital punishment for those who recant.

One of the Quran's most explicit statements on recantation is the 143rd verse of *Al-Baqarah*. The *Qiblah* was changed from Jerusalem to Mecca in the second year of *Hijrah*. Ibn Ishaq reports:

> And when the *Qiblah* was changed from Syria to the Kabah, Rifaa b. Qays, Qardam b.Amr, Kab b. al-Ashraf, Rafib Abu Rafi, al-Hajjaj b. Amr and an ally of Kab's, al-Rabi b. al-Rabi b. Abul-Huqayq and Kinana b. al-Rabi b. Abul Huqayq came to the Prophet[sa] and asked: 'Why have you turned your back on the *Qiblah* you used to face when you claimed to follow the religion of Abraham? If you returned to the *Qiblah* in Jerusalem we would follow you and declare you to be true.' Their sole intention was to seduce him from his religion. So God said: 'We

appointed the *Qiblah*, which you formerly observed, only to distinquish between he who will follow the Messenger and those who will not - to test and fetch them out. In truth, it was a hard test except for those whom Allah guided.[11]

The Quran prescribes no punishment for these recanters. And history records the punishment of no one who recanted after the change of the *Qiblah*.

Surah Al-Imran, which was revealed after the victory of Badr, 2AH/ AD/624, contains the following two verses which mention the recantation of some of the Jews of Medina:

O People of the Scripture: why do you confound the truth with falsehood and knowingly conceal the truth? (3:72)

And a party of the People of the Scripture says: 'Believe in that which has been revealed to those who believe at sunrise and disbelieve at sunset. In order that they may return.' (3:73)

Ibn Ishaq has given the names of those who hatched this plot:

Abdullah b. Sayf and Adiy b. Zayd and Al-Harith b. Auf agreed to pretend to believe in the message of Muhammad[sa] and his Companions at one time, deny it another to confuse them. The object was to get them to follow their example and give up their religion.[12]

None of these three Jews was punished.

Another reference is in *Al-Nisa*. It says: 'Those who believe then disbelieve, then believe again, then disbelieve and then increase their disbelief will never be forgiven by Allah, nor will He guide them to the way.'(4.138) A recanter cannot enjoy the repeated luxury of believing and disbelieving if the punishment is death. A dead man has no further chance of again believing and disbelieving.

The *sunnah*, the divinely inspired behaviour of the Holy Prophet[sa], is the second source of the *shari*.a And there is no penalty for conversion from Islam in the *sunnah* either. The names of those who were executed by the Prophet[sa] are preserved in the *sirah* and the *hadith* and the names of people who recanted and rejected Islam in his life are also preserved. A Bedouin Arab was converted to Islam by the Prophet[sa] and soon after suffered a fever while in Medina. He asked the Prophet[sa] to release him from his pledge. He made this request three times and was refused three times. He left Medina unmolested. The Prophet[sa], on hearing of his departure, observed: 'Medina is like a furnace which separates the dross from what is pure.'[13]

Ibn Ishaq reports that the Prophet[sa] had instructed his commanders when they entered Mecca to fight only those who resisted them. The only exceptions were the following criminals who were to be killed even if they were found wrapped within the curtains of the Kabah.[14]

1. Abdullah b. Sad b. Abi Sarah.
2, 3, 4. Abdullah b. Khatal of B. Tayam b. Ghalib and his two dancing girls, who used to sing satirical songs about Islam. One of them was Fartana, the name of the other is not given by Ibn Ishaq.
5. Al-Huwayrith b. Nuqaydh b. Wahb b. Abd b. Qusayy.
6. Miqyas b. Subabah.
7. Sarah, freed slave of one of the B. Abdul Muttalib.
8. Ikrama b. Abu Jahl.[15]

Abdullah b. Sad was one of the Prophet's[sa] scribes in Medina. He recanted and defected to the Meccan unbelievers. Since he wrote down the revelation, dictated by the Prophet[sa], and enjoyed a position of trust, his defection was bound to create confusion among the Quraish of Mecca about the authenticity of the revelation itself. After peace returned to Mecca, his foster brother, Uthman b. Affan, interceded with the Prophet[sa] on his behalf and he was pardoned.[16] Had there been a Quranic penalty for recantation, the Prophet[sa] could not have done so. The Prophet's[sa] policy on intercession in respect of *hadd* punishment is well illustrated by the incident of the *Makhzumi* woman who was found guilty of theft. When Usamah b. Zayd pleaded for her, the Prophet[sa] rebuked him and said: 'Do you intercede in respect of a punishment prescribed by Allah? Witness this: that if Fatima, daughter of Muhammad, were ever guilty of theft, I would certainly cut off her hand.'

Abdullah b. Khatal was sent by the Prophet[sa] to collect *zakat*, accomapnaied by an Ansar who served him. When they stopped, he ordered his companion to kill a goat for him and prepare some food before going to sleep. When he awoke the man had done nothing, so he killed him in anger and then recanted and defected to the Meccan Quraish.[17] He was executed for the murder of an Ansari Muslim by Said b. Hurayth al-Makhzumi and Abu Barzh al-Aslami.[18]

One of Ibn Khatal's two singing girls was killed for creating unrest by singing satirical songs; the other was pardoned.[19]

Al-Huwayrith b. Nuqaydh was in the party of Habbar b. al-Aswad b. al-Muttalib b. Asad who overtook the Prophet's[sa] daughter, Zaynab, when she was travelling from Mecca to Medina. Al-Huwayrith goaded Zaynab's camel. Zaynab was pregnant and had a miscarriage because of the attack and had to return to Mecca. The Prophet[sa] sent a number of people with orders that if they found Habbar b. al-Aswad or Al-Huwayrith they should kill them,[20] but Al-Huwayrith escaped. In another report, Hisham says that Al-Abbas b. Abd al-Muttalib put Fatima and Umm Kulthum, the two daughters of the Prophet[sa] on a camel to take them from Mecca to Medina. Al-Huwayrith goaded the beast so it threw the two women.[21] Finally, Ali killed him in Mecca.[22]

Maqees b. Subabah came to Medina from Mecca and said: 'I come to you as a Muslim seeking recompense for my brother, who was wrongly killed.' The Prophet[sa] ordered that he should be paid for his brother Hisham. Having received recompense, Maqees stayed with the Prophet[sa] for a while. But, as soon as he got an opportunity he killed his brother's slayer, recanted and defected to Mecca.[23] Maqees was executed by Numaylah b. Abdullah for killing an Ansar, on whose behalf the payment for killing his brother had already been paid.[24]

Sarah, who was accused of creating disorder, was not killed during the Prophet's[sa] lifetime.

Ikrama b. Abu Jahl fled to the Yemen. His wife, Umm Hakim, became a Muslim and asked immunity for him and this was granted by the Prophet[sa].[25]

There appears to be no evidence to show that the Prophet[sa] punished anyone for recantation from Islam.

The death of the Prophet[sa] in 11AH/AD632 confronted the young Muslim administration with a major crisis. Disorder broke out in parts of the peninsula and many tribes detached themselves from Medina by refusing to pay *zakat*. This movement is known as *Al-Riddah*. The main task of the Prophet's successor, Abu Bakr, was to put down this unrest. His first job, however, was to send the expedition the Holy Prophet[sa] had ordered before his death. So an army under the command of Usamah b. Zayd b. Harith was sent to the Syrian border on the second day after the proclamation of his caliphate.

After Usamah and his army had departed, most of the tribes fell away from Medina. Only Mecca, Medina and their surroundings remained loyal to the central administration. Muslim agents appointed to the rebel tribes by the Prophet[sa] just before his death were forced to flee their posts and to return to Medina. It was a full-fledged revolt.

Having decided to fight the rebels, Abu Bakr sent messengers to some loyal tribes calling them to come to his aid. While Abu Bakr was waiting for reinforcements, Kharjah b. Hism, led by Unaynah b. Hism al-Fazari and Al-Aqra b. Habis al-Tamimi, staged a surprise attack on the Muslims. The Muslims fled in confusion, but they re-assembled and counter-attacked Kharjah's men, who were defeated.

Before the skirmish at Dhu al-Qassa, a delegation of Arab tribes went to Medina to negotiate with Abu Bakr over the question of *zakat*, but Abu Bakr refused. Some early and prominent *muhajirun* disagreed with Abu Bakr's decision to fight those who withheld the *zakat*. That these tribes were anxious to negotiate showed they had not recanted, and did not want to sever their relations with Medina, yet were not prepared to accept Medina's control over them. The issue was not belief in Allah and His Prophet[sa], but the *zakat* (tax). A group of well-known friends led by Umar objected to Abu Bakr's decision to fight the rebels. Umar is reported to have said to Abu Bakr: 'What right do you have to fight these people? The Prophet[sa] has said, "I was ordered to fight people until they say there is no God but Allah. If they say this, they safeguard themselves and their property from me."'[26]

After the departure of the delegation from Medina, Abu Bakr gathered the Muslims of Medina and addressed them as follows:

'The delegation has observed just how few of you there are in Medina. You do not know whether they will attack you by day or night. Their vanguard is only a stone's throw from Medina. They wanted us to accept their proposals and make an agreement with them, but we have rejected their request. So make ready for their attack.' Within three days they attacked Medina.[27]

The war of *Riddah* caused a great deal of bloodshed. It was inexplicable to the subsequent historians of the Arabian state that after the death of Muhammad[sa] so many wars were necessary on Arabian soil; they accounted for this fact by a *Ridda*,[28] a religious movement against Islam. The jurists, who had failed to find Quranic or *sunnah* authority for the execution of Muslims accused of *kufr*, or war, against opposing Muslim political powers, accepted the assumption without more ado.

Discussing the legality of Abu Bakr's war against Muslim rebels, Imam Al-Shafi'i says: '*Riddah* is falling back from a previously adopted religion into disbelief and refusing to fulfil previously accepted responsibility.'[29] Recantation is not enough. It must be aggravated by allegations of the breach of an agreement. Ibn Abi al-Hadid, a scholar of a very different school, in his commentary of the *Nahj al-Balaghah*, clarified the matter when he said: 'The tribes which refused to pay *zakat* were not recanters, they were called so, metaphorically, by the Companions of the Prophet[sa].'[30]

According to Wellhausen, *Riddah* was a break with the leadership in Medina and not with Islam itself. Most of the tribes wanted to continue worshipping Allah, but without paying tax. Caetani agrees with

Wellhausen and says the *Riddah* was not a movement of recantation and that these wars were purely about politics. Becker, following Wellhausen and Caetani, concludes:

> The sudden death of Mahomet gave new support to the centrifugal tendencies. The character of the whole movement, as it forces itself on the notice of the historian, was of course hidden from contemporaries. Arabia would have sunk into particularism if the necessity caused by the secession of *Al-Riddah* had not developed in the State of Medina an energy which carried all before it. The fight against the *Ridda* was not a fight against apostates, the objection was not to Islam, *per se*, but to the tribute which had to be paid to Medina; the fight was for political supremacy over Arabia. [31]

Bernard Lewis makes it quite clear that *Riddah* 'represents a distortion of the real significance of events by the theologically coloured outlook of later historians'. He goes on to say:

> The refusal of the tribes to recognise the succession of Abu Bakr was, in effect, not a relapse by converted Muslims to their previous paganism, but the simple and automatic termination of a political contract by the death of one of the parties. The tribes nearest to Medina had in fact been converted and their interests were so closely identified with those of the *umma* that their separate history has not been recorded. For the rest, the death of Muhammad automatically severed their bonds with Medina, and the parties resumed their liberty of action. They felt in no way bound by the election of Abu Bakr in which they had taken no part, and at once suspended both tribute and treaty relations. In order to re-establish the hegemony of Medina, Abu Bakr had to make new treaties. [32]

Ali was assassinated in 661. With him went the concept of a Muslim ruler who combined the functions of head of state and of religion. The dynastic reign of the Ummayyads (661-750), the political rulers of Islam, began with Muawiyah. They had none of the religious outlook of the pious caliphs and were regarded more or less as secular kings. As guardians of the *sharia* the *ulema* came to occupy a position comparable in many ways to that of the clergy after the conversion of Constantine. Like the clergy in medieval Europe, they were respected for learning and piety and their support was sought to legalise the political power of a despot or unpopular ruler. They also acted as the leaders of the opposition and tried to influence political power rather than assume it themselves.

Political and social revolts were now justified in religious terms and dynastic struggles over political power soon hardened into deep rifts in religious doctrine. Kharijism and Shiism, the two main movements that split off from the main body after the assassination of the third caliph, Uthman (644), originated during a struggle for succession. Kharijites were the first Muslims to suggest that a grave sinner no longer remained Muslim. They were also the first to proclaim *jihad* against Muslims who, according to them, were not true believers, and originally belonged to Ali's party; they left him, however, over a disagreement about arbitration between him and Muawiyah, intended to settle their differences arising out of Uthman's murder. They said: 'judgement belongs to Allah alone' and not to human tribunals. Kharijites were key figures in the development of dogma. They were particular about a Muslim's qualifications and his attitude towards his fellow men, Muslim or non-Muslim. This group was the first distinct sect to appear in Islam, and was also the first to reject the principle of justification by faith. They maintained that a grave sinner no longer remained a Muslim and could not re-enter the faith; instead, he should be killed with his family. They considered all non-Kharijites to be outlaws and non-Muslim. As we saw earlier, the Prophet[sa] knew the *munafiqun* of Medina and their leader, Abdullah b. Ubayy, and yet he took no action against him. He did not judge the quality of a Muslim's faith.

The Kharijites conflicted directly with the teaching of the Quran and the *sunnah* of the Prophet[sa]. Their declaration that 'judgement belongs to Allah alone' (*la hukma illa lillah*)[33] was in total contradiction to the *sunnah*. The Prophet[sa] appointed Sad b. Muadh as *hakam* to decide the fate of the Jewish tribe of B. Qurayzah and his sentence was carried out.[34] Commenting on the *Sahih Muslim* report of Sad's judgement, Al-Nawawi (d. 676AH/AD127) said: 'In their disputes Muslims are allowed to resort to *tahkim*'.[35] In fact, if two Muslim groups are at war, it is the duty of other Muslims to make peace between them. The Quran says: 'All believers are brothers, and be mindful of your duty to Allah that you may be shown mercy.' (49.11) Declaring Muslims to be 'disbelievers' and then punishing them just because their standards are different from the standards of a certain religious authority - *takfir* - is alien to Islam. The Prophet[sa] himself defined a Muslim as one who declares faith in the Unity of Allah and the prophethood of Muhammad[sa].[36] This is the only definition by which a Muslim can be judged. Discussing the subject of *takfir*, Bernard Lewis says:

> Even open rebellion did not automatically involve *takfir*. In 923 the chief Qadi ibn Buhal refused to denounce the Carmathian rebels as unbelievers since they began their letters with invocations to God and

70

the Prophet and were therefore, on the face of it, Muslims. The Shafi'i law insists that the sectarian, even in revolt, is entitled to be treated as a Muslim; that is to say, his family and property are respected, and that he cannot be summarily despatched or sold into slavery once he becomes a prisoner.[37]

Takfir[38] was, however, founded by jurists. As we saw earlier, it was a *Kharijite* excuse for denouncing Ali. But having adopted this *Kharijite* innovation, the jurists could not arrive at an agreed definition of a Muslim.

To comb 1300 years of Islamic history to find the number of Muslims executed because of their conversion from Islam would prove futile. There were unsuccessful attempts to execute Maimonides in Cairo,[39] the Maronite Amir Yunis in Lebanon,[40] and to persecute Rashid-ud-Din in Tabriz,[41] but such instances were very rare. In Mughal India, there is only one recorded case. A Portuguese friar had embraced Islam and then reverted to his former faith. He was executed at Aurangabad.[42] The reasons for his execution were political, not religious. The friar was under strong suspicion of spying for the Portuguese under the cover of Islam.

Jadd ibn Dirham was put to death on the orders of Hisham b. Abd al-Malik in Kufa or Wasit in 124 or 125AH/AD746 or 747. He was accused of having advanced the Mutazili doctrines of the created Quran and of freewill. In 167 or 168AH/AD788 the Iraqi poet Bashir b. Burd was accused of *zandaqah*, beaten and thrown into a swamp in Batiha. Al-Husain b. Mansur al-Hallaj was executed in 309AH/AD930 for blasphemy because he claimed to have substantial union with God (*hulul*). Shihab-ul-Din Yahya al-Suhrawardi was put to death on the orders of Al-Malik al-Zahir (578AH/AD1199). His crime was to regard all that lives, moves or has its being as truth and he even based his proof of God upon the symbol of light.

The seventeenth-century martyr was Muhammad Said Sarmad. Born of Jewish parents at Kashan, Sarmad was a rabbi before embracing Islam. A great Persian poet, he was a monist and denied the existence of matter. He was executed in the reign of Aurangzib (reigned 1658-1707). His *mazar* (tomb) which is opposite the Jami Masjid in Delhi, attracts daily hundreds of Muslims, offering flowers and *Fatihah*.

In Afghanistan, two Ahmadis were executed for accepting the claim of Mirza Ghulam Ahmad[as] of Qadiyan to be the Promised Messiah, Sahibzadah Abdul Latif, who performed the coronation ceremony of Amir Habib Ullah Khan, was stoned to death in 1903 and Maulwi Nimat

Ullah in 1924. Both were given the chance of renouncing the claims of Mirza Ghulam Ahmad[as], but they refused.

Muhammad Mahmud Taha was executed in the Sudan in 1985. He believed the Medinite part of the Quranic law was no longer applicable.

Significantly, the Ottoman sultan, though the head of a religious empire and caliph of all Muslims, did not order the execution of Baha Ullah (1817-92) for *irtidad*. Baha Ullah declared himself to be the Promised One, foretold by Bab,[43] and founded Bahaism as a religion. Bahaism was and is totally different from Islam. It declares that the arrival of Baha Ullah makes the Quran and the teachings of Muhammad - may peace and blessings of Allah be upon him - out of date. Baha Ullah was jailed in Akka (Acre) near Haifa, then in Palestine, now Israel. But when Sabbatai Zevi (1627-76), a Jewish mystic, proclaimed himself the Messiah in 1648, the Shaykh-ul-Islam of the Ottoman Empire ordered his execution. He was arrested, recanted from his claim simply to escape death, and embraced Islam. Baha Ullah claimed to be a new manifestation of God and left Islam, but was not executed despite his apostasy because he was not a danger to law and order in the Ottoman Empire.

As we have already seen, the concept of apostasy is alien to Islam and there is no punishment in this world for recanting. But the *ulema* who appeared before the Court of Inquiry, constituted under the Punjab Act II of 1954 to enquire into the Punjab disturbances of 1953, asserted that 'apostasy in an Islamic state is punishable by death'. They were:

> Maulana Abul Hasanat Sayyad Muhammad Ahmad Qadri, President, Jamiat-ul-Ulamai-Pakistan, Punjab; Maulana Ahmad Ali, Sadr Jamiat-ul-Ulama-e-Islam, West Pakistan; Maulana-Abul Ala Maududi, founder and ex-Amir-i-Jamaati Islami, Pakistan; Mufti Muhammad Idris, Jami Ashrafia, Lahore, and member, Jamiat-ul-Ulamai-Pakistan; Maulana Daud Ghaznavi, President, Jamaati Ahl-i-Hadith, Maghribi Pakistan; Maulana Abdul Haleem Qasimi, Jamiat-ul-Ulamai-Islam, Punjab; and Mr Ibrahim Ali Chishti.[44]

Commenting on this assertion, the Court of Inquiry observed:

> According to this doctrine, Chaudhri Zafrullah Khan must be executed if he has not inherited his present religious beliefs, but has elected of his own free will to be an Ahmadi. And the same fate should befall Deobandis and Wahabis, (including Maulana Muhammad Shafi Deobandi, member, Board of Talimat-i-Islami attached to the Constituent Assembly of Pakistan, and Maulana Daud Ghaznavi) if any one of the *ulema* (shown perched on every leaf of a beautiful tree in the *fatwa* (Ex. D.E. 14)

were the head of such an Islamic state. And if Maulana Muhammad Shafi Deobandi were the head of the state, he would exclude those who have been pronounced Deobandis to be *kafirs* from Islam. He would then execute them, if they came within the definition of *murtadd*, namely, if they had changed and not inherited their religious views.

The genuineness of the *fatwa* (Ex. D.E. 13) by the Deobandis, which says that Ithnashri Shias are *kafirs* and *murtadds*) was questioned in the course of our inquiry. But Maulana Muhammad Shafi examined the subject from Deoband and received from the records of that institution the copy of a *fatwa* signed by all the teachers of the Darul Ulloom, including Maulana Muhammad Shafi himself. The records say, in effect, that those who do not believe in the *sahabiyyat* of Hazrat Siddiq Akbar and who are *qazif* of Hazrat Aisha Siddiqa and have been guilty of *tehrif* of the Quran, are *kafirs*. This opinion is also shared by Mr Ibrahim Ali Ghishti who knows and has studied this subject. He thinks the Shias are *kafirs* because they believe that Hazrat Ali shared the prophethood with our Holy Prophet[sa]. He refused to answer the question of whether a Sunni who changed his views and agrees with the Shias is guilty of *irtidad*, thus deserving death. According to the Shias, all Sunnis are *kafirs* and Ahl-i-Quran - persons who consider *hadith* unreliable and therefore not binding - are also *kafirs*. So are all independent thinkers. The net result is that neither Shias nor Sunnis nor Deobandis nor Ahl-i-Hadith nor Brelvis are Muslims. And that, if the government of the state is run by a party which considers the other party to be *kafirs*, then any change from one view to another must result in the death penalty.

It does not take much imagination to judge the consequences of this doctrine when it is remembered that no two *ulema* have ever agreed before us on the correct definition of a Muslim. Indeed, if all their definitions are taken in total, the grounds on which someone may be indicted for apostasy would be too numerous even to count.[45]

CHAPTER 7

PUNISHMENT FOR APOSTASY

In earlier chapters we have given numerous references from the Holy Quran and the history of Islam to expose the fallacy that Islam prescribes any corporal punishment for those who renounce Islam as their faith. We examined at length the most common arguments presented by the advocates of death for apostasy, namely the report of Ikramah and the incident of *zakat* in Hazrat Abu Bakr's time. Some other arguments are examined in this chapter.

It is difficult to assess whether the concept of coercion in Islam had its birth on Islamic soil or was the child of the orientalists' imagination and was later on transferred to the lap of Islam. Having examined this in the light of Islamic history, I honestly believe that the idea first took root in the Islamic world itself and that it is wrong of us to blame the orientalists for having initiated it. They picked it up from the Muslims: before the orientalists were even born, the idea seems to have been present in medieval Islamic thought. It originated in the late Umayyad dynasty. Throughout the Abbaside period, the idea continued to flourish and was further strengthened because the Abbaside sovereigns wanted to use force not only against the enemies of Islam but also against their own people. A licence for this was not infrequently sought from Muslim scholars under their influence. The concept has therefore arisen from the conduct and policies of the post-Khalifat-i Rashida[1] Muslim governments of Baghdad.

Looking on from the outside, Western scholars believed that this was an Islamic teaching, but the fact was that it was not Islamic at all. It was the basis of the behaviour of some Muslim governments. We should remember that the idea had its birth in an age when all over the world the use of force for the spread of influence and ideology was a common feature and no exception was taken to this.

It is clear that the allegation that Islam advocates the use of force for the spread of its ideology does not originate from a study of the sources of Islamic teachings but from a study of the conduct of some Muslim states. Now that a new era has dawned in which all the Islamic literature and traditions are available to us and the Holy Quran has been translated into so many languages - when Western scholars have direct access to the sources of Islamic teachings - their persistence in making the allegation is unjustified. They should go to the sources and study the teachings of the Holy Quran, the traditions and the conduct of the Holy Prophet, Muhammad[sa], himself.

This work is an attempt to examine the whole issue, not in the light of how Muslims of a certain era behaved, but in the light of the fundamental teachings of the Holy Quran and the exposition of those teachings by the words of the Holy Prophet[sa] and by his conduct.

The tendency to judge teachings by the conduct of their followers has often misled people about the original teachings. It is universally observed that after a while all religions lose their influence on the conduct of their adherents. For illustrations of this, study the behaviour of the Buddhists of today or of earlier eras, study the behaviour of the Hindu governments, and so on and so forth; it often has no relationship whatsoever with the original teachings. In particular, politics must not be confused with religion; political behaviour of a nation should not be treated as a mirror reflecting the teachings of the religion which its people are supposed to follow.

It is against this background that we examine the arguments presented by the advocates of death as a punishment for apostasy.

Definition of an apostate

The Holy Quran states:

They will not stop fighting you until they turn you back from your faith, if they can. The works of those from among you who turn back from their faith and die in a state of disbelief shall be vain in this world and the next. These are the inmates of the fire, therin shall they abide. (2. 218)

This means that whoever, out of fear of the sword (or the pain of punishment), decides to abjure Islam has a fundamental right to do so but no one else has the right to declare him to be an apostate. The right to declare himself to be an apostate lies only with him. Nowhere in the Holy Quran has this right been granted to others. That is to say, one is free to renounce one's own religion but has no right to impose renunciation of religion on others. According to Islamic teachings, an apostate, therefore, cannot be manufactured by religious scholars or the clergy or any non-tolerant individual or government.

75

The Holy Quran also states: 'Surely, those who have turned away after guidance has been made manifest to them have been deceived by Satan who has beguiled them with false hopes.' (47.26)

Other verses from the Holy Quran on apostasy

The Holy Quran says:

O ye who believe, whoso from among you turns back from his religion let him remember that in place of such a person, Allah will soon bring a people whom He will love and who will love Him, who will be kind and considerate towards the believers and firm and unyielding towards the disbelievers. They will strive hard in the cause of Allah and will not at all take to heart the reproaches of fault finders. That is Allah's grace; He bestows it upon whosoever He pleases. Allah is the Lord of vast bounty, All-Knowing. (5.55)

Whoso disbelieves in Allah after he has believed, excepting the case of one who is forced to make a declaration of disbelief while his heart rests securely in faith, but one who opens his mind wide to disbelief; on him is Allah's wrath and he shall have a grievous punishment. (16.107)

Those who believe, then disbelieve, then again believe, then disbelieve and thereafter go on increasing in disbelief, Allah will never forgive them, nor guide them to any way of deliverance. (4.138)

Muhammad is but a Messenger; of a surety, all Messengers before him have passed away. If then, he dies or be slain, will you turn back on your heels? He who turns back on his heels shall not harm Allah a whit. Allah will certainly reward the grateful. (3.145)

No corporal punishment can be understood to have been mentioned by any stretch of imagination in the foregoing passages from the Holy Quran.

Surah Al-Tauba

In a desperate search for at least one verse in the Holy Quran which might lend support for death as a punishment for apostasy, recourse has been made to verses 12 and 13 of Chapter 9 (*Surah Al-Tauba*). We quote below verses 3-14 of that chapter. These speak for themselves and defy all attempts on the part of anyone who would have them understood differently:

3. This is a public proclamation on the part of Allah and His Messenger on the day of the Great Pilgrimage, that Allah is free of all obligation to the idolaters, and so is His Messenger. So now, having witnessed this Sign, if you will repent and make peace, it will be better for you; but if you turn away, then know that you cannot frustrate Allah's design. Warn the disbelievers of a painful chastisement.

4. Excepting those of them with whom you have a pact and who have not defaulted in any respect, nor supported anyone against you. Carry out the obligations you have assumed towards them till the end of their terms. Surely, Allah loves those who are mindful of their obligations.

5. When the period of four months during which hostilities are suspended expires, without the idolaters having settled the terms of peace with you, resume fighting with them and kill them wherever you find them and make them prisoners and beleaguer them, and lie in wait for them at every place of ambush. Then if they repent and observe prayers and pay the *zakat*, leave them alone. Surely, Allah is Most Forgiving, Ever Merciful.

6. If any one of the idolaters seeks asylum with thee, grant him asylum so that he may hear the Word of Allah; then convey him to a place of security for him, for they are a people who lack knowledge.

7. How could there be a guarantee for the idolaters on the part of Allah and His Messenger, except in favour of those with whom you entered into an express treaty at the Sacred Mosque? So long as they carry out their obligations thereunder, you must carry out your obligations. Surely, Allah loves those who are mindful of their obligations.

8. How can there be a guarantee for the others who, if they were to prevail against you, would have no regard for any tie of kinship or pact in respect of you. They seek to please you with words, while their hearts repudiate them; most of them are perfidious.

9. They have bartered the Sign of Allah for small gains and hindered people from His way. Evil indeed is that which they have done.

10. They show no regard for any tie of kinship or any pact in respect of a believer. It is they who are the transgressors.

11. If they repent and observe prayer and pay the *zakat*, then they are your brethren in faith. We expound our commandments for a people who know.

12. But if they break faith after pledging it and ridicule your religion, then fight these leaders of disbelief that they may desist, for they have no regard for their pledged word.

13. Will you not fight a people who have violated their oaths, who plotted to turn out the Messenger from his home, and who were the first to start hostilities against you? Do you fear them? It is Allah Who is Most

Worthy that you should fear Him, if you are believers.
14. Fight them: Allah will punish them at your hands, and will humiliate them, and will help you to overcome them, and will relieve the minds of the believers of fear and distress.

Those who deduce from verses 12 and 13 that the punishment for apostasy is death offer no explanation of the contradiction this creates with numerous other verses. These verses relate to the period after the migration from Mecca to Medina (see verse 3) when the Quraish of Mecca had embarked upon hostilities to wipe out Islam by force.

The advocates of capital punishment for apostasy should remember that these verses refer to idolaters who have broken their pledges and ridicule religion; there is no mention of people renouncing their faith. They have broken their pledge after their firm commitment to it. Those who have become hostile to your religion are the first to initiate hostilities against you. The permission for you to fight them is restricted to their leaders whose covenants are worthless and false. The permission is given in order to stop them from entering into hostile acts against you.

This is the true meaning of these verses which have been misconstrued by the advocates of capital punishment. There is not even the remotest reference to people who renounce their faith being forced to become Muslims. The same people are discussed in another part of the Holy Quran:

It may be that Allah will bring about amity between you and those with whom you are at enmity. Allah has the power; Allah is Most Forgiving, Ever Merciful. Allah does not forbid you to be kind and act equitably towards those who have not fought you because of your religion, and who have not driven you forth from your homes. Surely Allah loves those who are equitable. Allah only forbids you that you make friends with those who have fought against you because of your religion and have driven you out of your homes and have aided others in driving you out. Whoso makes friends with them, those are the transgressors. (60.8-10)

Temporary disbelief

Another verse of the Holy Quran states:

A section of the people of the Book urge some from among themselves: why not affirm, in the early part of the day, belief in that which has been revealed unto the believers and repudiate it in the latter part of the day, perchance they may turn away from their faith. (3.73)

The people of the Book mentioned in this verse are the Jews of Medina. Theirs was a Jewish tactic to create doubt among the Muslims in the hope that some of them might thereby by beguiled into repudiating Islam. How could it be possible for the Jews to have enacted this plan if death was a penalty for apostasy? Had anyone been executed for commiting this crime, that would have been a deterrent for others who would not follow in their footsteps.

The advocates of the death penalty urge that this verse merely refers to a Jewish philosophy which was never put into practice by them. Even if it was merely a philosophy, this verse is conclusive proof of there being no punishment in this world for apostasy because the Jews could never have conceived the idea had there been such a punishment. Moreover, it is wrong to say that the idea was a hypothetical case; the books of tradition mention that it was put into practice by twelve Jewish divines of Khaibar and Urainah.[2](See also p.65)

All commentaries agree that this chapter of the Holy Quran was revealed between the victory of Mecca and the demise of the Holy Prophet[sa]. This conclusively proves that the Jews put it into practice after Islam became firmly established in Arabia. How could the Jews ever think of such a suicidal and insane strategy if death was prescribed as a punishment for apostasy? How could they encourage Muslims to follow their faith by affirming it during the day and repudiating it at the end of the day if they knew that the Muslims would be executed for changing their faith?

Traditions

The advocates of capital punishment for apostasy misconstrue out of all proportion the traditions narrated about the Holy Prophet[sa]. Traditions lend no support to their thesis. On the contrary, there are many traditions which clearly show that there is no punishment for apostasy in this life.

However, for the sake of completeness, we set out those traditions which are most often cited by advocates of capital punishment for apostasy.

a) Abu Qalabah reports on the authority of Anas that the Holy Prophet[sa] told the people of Akal or Uraynah to go and stay among his she-camels outside Medina. These people killed the keeper of the camels and ran away with the herd. Although it is true that these people had become apostates, their punishment was not a result of their apostasy but of their murder of the keeper of the she-camels. (See also page 34.)

b) Whereas Ibn Khatal, who was without doubt one of the four executed on the fall of Mecca, was an apostate, he had also committed the crime of murdering his travelling companion. His execution was, therefore, obviously ordered as a result of his having been convicted as a murderer. (See also page 66.)

c) Another incident is that of Maqees b. Sababah who killed an Ansar in revenge for Hisham, his brother, who was accidentally killed during the campaign of Zeeqard. Thereafter, Maqees became an apostate. He was executed on account of the murder of the Ansar. (See also page 67.)

In each one of the above incidents, the executed person had committed murder. The three people had also happened to renounce their faith, but how can anyone shut their eyes to the murders and attribute their executions to their acts of apostasy?

d) The advocates of capital punishment for apostasy rely heavily on a tradition which mentions the execution of a woman for apostasy. This tradition is most unreliable, to say the least. The truth of the matter is that the Holy Prophet[sa] never ordered the execution of a woman on account of her apostasy. The well-known treatise of jurisprudence, *Hedayah*, sets out the following:

> The Holy Prophet[sa] forbade the killing of women for apostasy, because the principle of punitive regulations is that in such cases the penalty should be left for the hereafter, as a penalty imposed in this life would contravene the purpose of apostasy, being a trial calling to account what pertains to God alone. This can be departed from only when the object in view is to restrain the person concerned from continuing hostilities (during times of war). As women, by their very nature, are not capable of fighting, a woman apostate cannot be punished in any case.

Strangely enough, scholars like Maududi, who might be supposed to be fully aware of serious flaws in the reliability of these traditions, still adhere to weak traditions which have been rejected by most eminent Muslim scholars.

e) The incident of Abdullah Bin Sad has already been quoted on page 66. Had there been any Quranic penalty for apostasy, how could the Holy Prophet's[sa] words to the effect that no one is above the law would be a clear reminder of his strict observance of God's laws. If death was the punishment for apostasy, how could the Holy Prophet[sa] disobey the commandments of God?

Companions

We have observed that neither the Holy Quran nor any reliable traditions of the Holy Prophet[sa] lend any support to those who advocate capital punishment for apostasy. But those advocates have some other tricks up their sleeves. It is necessary to examine their remaining arguments at greater length. Those arguments are based on the opinions of the Companions of the Holy Prophet[sa], and not directly on his own personal judgement. Let it be known at the outset that observations or opinions of Companions[as] can only be a commentary; they have no right to be treated with as much respect as an injunction of the Holy Quran. At best they can only be regarded as an opinion.

a) The incident of the widespread apostasy in relation to the payment of *zakat* has been discussed (pages 69-72). The Abs and the Zubyan were the tribes which initiated hostilities by attacking Medina. Hazrat Abu Bakr fought them before the return of Osama from his expedition. The apostates were the aggressors. They not only refused to pay *zakat*, but also took up the sword against the Muslims. Thus they rebelled against the Islamic state, slaughtered the Muslims amongst them by burning some alive and mutilated those they had killed.[3] Those who advocate execution for apostasy on the authority of this incident are either ignorant of the facts or deliberately seeking to mislead people by playing down the killing of innocent Muslims by the rebels.

b) The advocates then pose the question that if there was no punishment for apostasy, why was Musailmah the imposter not left alone? The truth is that Musailmah aspired to political power. He had accompanied Abu Hanifa and offered to the Holy Prophet[sa] his submission subject to his being nominated as his successor. The Holy Prophet[sa] told Musailmah that he would not yield him even a twig of a date palm tree. Musailmah returned and claimed that half of Arabia belonged to him. He sent a letter to the Holy Prophet[sa] in which he claimed: 'I have been appointed your partner in authority.' The Holy Prophet[sa] responded by quoting to him verse 129 of chapter 7 of the Holy Quran.[4] After Musailmah's claim of prophethood, he captured Habeeb b. Zaid, a Companion of the Holy Prophet[sa], dismembered him limb from limb, and then burned his remains. The advocates of capital punishment ignore this gruesome murder and claim that apostasy was the only crime attributable to Musailmah. Had he not commited murder, would he have been killed for the crime of apostasy alone? Was he not brought to justice for the murder and for the mayhem and disorder which he created in the land? There is not the slightest shred of evidence that having heard of Musailmah's rejection of his prophethood, the Holy Prophet[sa] condemned Musailmah to death or exhorted any of his Companions to kill him. Having failed to find evidence of any specific condemnation by the Holy Prophet[sa], Maulana

Maududi had to seek recourse in a wish which the Holy Prophet[sa] is said to have expressed during his dying moments, that Musailmah should be done away with. Had there been such a wish, it is impossible for us to believe that the Holy Prophet's[sa] first successor, Hazrat Abu Bakr, would have ignored it and not sent an expedition in compliance with the wish of the Holy Prophet[sa]. Why did Hazrat Abu Bakr wait until the time when Musailmah himself took the offensive and openly rebelled against the Muslims? We find that Musailmah mustered a force of 40,000 warriors of Banu Hanifa alone when he fought Khalid b. Walid. Musailmah initiated hostilities and moved against Medina. It was only then that Hazrat Abu Bakr gave orders to march against him on account of his rebellion and his gruesome murder of Habeeb bin Zaid.[5]

c) Another incident cited is that of Tulaiha, another pretender to prophethood. Again, he was not just a pretender but had murdered Ukasha b. Mohsin and Thabit b. Aqram Ansari. Before Khalid b. Walid commenced battle with him, he sent an emissary to Tulaiha to agree peace terms and avoid bloodshed. The advocates of capital punishment overlook the fact that if there had been capital punishment for apostasy, there was no point in sending an emissary offering forgiveness to Tulaiha.[6]

d) A similar case is that of Aswad Anasi who raised the standard of rebellion with his apostasy. He killed the Muslim governor of Yemen, Shahr b. Bazan, forcibly married his widow and made himself ruler of Yemen. When the Holy Prophet[sa] learned of his rebellion, he sent a letter to Muaz b. Jabal and the Muslims to oppose Aswad Anasi, who was subsequently killed in a skirmish with the Muslims. (News of his death arrived one day after the demise of the Holy Prophet[sa].)[7]

e) Similarly, Laqbeet b. Malik Azdi became an apostate and claimed to be a prophet. He expelled Jafar and Abad who had been appointed as functionaries in Oman.[8] He, like all these claimants to prophethood, had no concern with religion. He had his own political axe to grind. His search for political domination was through open rebellion against the Islamic state he lived in, so the question of apostasy is irrelevant here. Let us suppose for a moment that all these people had not recanted their faith but had merely rebelled against the Muslim state. The state would have had to take the step of quelling the rebellion; for the crime of creating disorder in the land, the Holy Quran prescribes capital punishment. That punishment is not for apostasy.

f) The advocates of capital punishment for apostacy cite also the case of Umm Qarfah, a woman who became an apostate during the time of

Hazrat Abu Bakr. She had thirty sons whom she constantly exhorted to fight the Muslims. She paid the price for her treason and for her complicity in murder, not on account of her apostasy.[9]

g) The case of Hazrat Ali fighting the Khawarij is often cited. The Khawarij created disorder in the land, killed Muslim men and women, the governor appointed by Hazrat Ali, his female slave, and also Ali's emissary.[10] (This incident has been discussed on p.70.)

h) Reference needs to be made to the appointments of Muaz b. Jabal and Abu Musa Ashari, each as governor of a part of Yemen. As they were about to leave, the Holy Prophet[sa] instructed them: 'Make things easy for people and do not put them into difficulty. Talk to them cheerfully and not in a manner that might repel them' One day Muaz came to meet Abu Musa Ashari and noticed a person sitting there who had been secured with a rope. When Muaz enquired about this he was told that that person was a Jew who had become a Muslim and then became an apostate. The narrator adds that for the past two to three months the Muslims had reasoned with him in order to persuade him to become a Muslim but to no avail. Muaz declared that he would not dismount until the person had been executed and observed that this was the judgement of God and His Messenger. This last remark indicates no more than his personal opinion of what he understood to be the Will of God and His prophet. Such opinions carry no weight in law unless they are completely substantiated by references which verify the claim. (This principle is elaborated subsequently in this chapter.)

Now let us examine the reliability of this tradition. Muaz's remark contradicts the instruction of the Holy Prophet[sa] to make things easy for people and not in a manner which might repel them. To place reliance on one tradition without investigating Muaz's understanding of Islam on a key issue where human rights are involved is sheer absurdity.

Considerable doubt prevails regarding this tradition, the chain of narrators and their authenticity. Wherever such disputes arise, the tradition is rejected outright. It should be remembered that these traditions were compiled some three to four centuries after the advent of Islam and that, over a passage of time, memories are prone to error. According to one tradition, the Jew was beheaded upon Muaz's instructions.[11] In the second tradition, Muaz himself beheaded the Jew.[12] When such fundamental differences occur in a key incident, how can anyone accept the authenticity of these traditions? People may forget what someone said, but if they were eye-witnesses they would at least remember what ultimately happened to the 'apostate' in question.

Next we turn to a tradition which has obtained much attention because it is strongly emphasised and relied upon by the school advocating capital punishment for apostasy. This has deliberately been deferred to the end of this chapter so that justice may be done to it without interfering with the general flow of the subject matter.

Before a detailed examination of this tradition, a few words concerning the application of certain principles accepted by Islamic scholars throughout the ages would not be out of place. These principles help to resolve controversies concerning the apparent contradiction between the Holy Quran and *hadith* (tradition) on the one hand and some traditions *vis-à-vis* other traditions.

1. The Word of God stands supreme.

2. This is followed by the actual practices of the Holy Prophet of Islam[sa]. This is known as *sunnah*.

3. This is followed by *hadith*, the words reported to be those of the Holy Prophet[sa].

a) If the authenticity of the words of the Holy Prophet[sa] is established unquestionably, the words concerned are words put into the mouth of the Holy Prophet[sa] by God Almighty. Where there is no apparent contradiction between the word of the Holy Prophet[sa] and the Quran, the tradition may be accepted as authentic.

b) There are no two opinions regarding the accepted fact that whenever any so-called tradition attributed to the Holy Prophet of Islam[sa] contradicts any clear injunction of the Holy Quran, such a tradition is rejected as false and is not accepted as the word of the Holy Prophet[sa].

c) If such a tradition does not glaringly violate any injunction of the Holy Quran and there is room for compromise, then ideally an attempt should be made to search for a suitable compromise before the final rejection of the tradition.

d) In attempting to reconcile a tradition attributed to the Holy Prophet[sa] with the Holy Quran, it must always be borne in mind that the clear teachings of the Holy Quran are not to be compromised for the sake of a so-called tradition, but a genuine attempt is to be made to find an explanation of the tradition. Therefore in all cases of doubt, the tradition is put to the anvil of the Holy Quran and judged accordingly.

e) If there is no contradiction between the Holy Quran and *hadith*, then their mutual merit of credibility would be determined according to the reliability of the sources and the chain of narrators.

f) Such a tradition will also be compared with other authentic and widely accepted traditions to make sure that the tradition does not conflict with other traditions.

g) Lastly, another reliable method of investigating the credibility of a tradition is to study its internal evidence critically. If the contents of the tradition clash with the image of the Holy Prophet of Islam[sa] which has emerged from a study of his conduct and bearing throughout his life, then such a tradition would be rejected as a false attribution to the Holy Prophet[sa] or as being against the principles of logic and common sense.

In the light of the above principles, let us examine[13] the tradition in question.

Tradition

It is recorded that:

> Ikramah relates that he heard that some Zindeeqs were presented before Hazrat Ali whereupon he directed the burning alive of these people. Ibn Abbas stated that had it been him, he would not have ordered this because the Holy Prophet[sa] had said that the torment of the fire may only be decreed by God but the Prophet had also said, 'Slay whosoever changes his religion'[14]

This tradition, with some variation, may also be found in Tirmidhi, Abu Daud, Al-Nisai and Ibn Majah's compilations.

Contradiction with the Holy Quran

It is not possible for a fair-minded person to reconcile the following verses of the Holy Quran with this tradition:

2.57, 100, 109, 218, 257, 273	22.40
3.21, 73, 86-92, 145	24.55
4.83, 138, 139, 146	25.42-4
5.55, 62, 91-3, 99-100	26.117
6.67, 105-8, 126	28.57
7.124-9	29.19
9.11-14	39.30-42
10.100-9	40.26, 27
13.41	42.7, 8, 48, 49
15.10	47.26
16.83, 105-7, 126	50.46
17.55	51.57
18.30	64.9-13

19.47   66.7
20.72-4   88.22-3

Some of the verses listed have been quoted earlier. For the sake of further elucidation the following passage is set out:

Whoso seeks a religion other than Islam, it shall not be accepted from him, and in the life to come he shall be among the losers. How shall Allah guide a people who have disbelieved after having believed and who had borne witness that the Messenger is true and to him clear proofs had come? Allah guides not the wrongdoers. Of such the punishment is that on them shall be the curse of Allah and of angels and of men, all together; thereunder shall they abide. Their punishment shall not be lightened nor shall they be granted respite; except in the case of those who repent thereafter and amend. Surely, Allah is Most Forgiving, Ever Merciful. Those who disbelieve after having believed, and then continue to advance in disbelief, their repentance shall not be accepted. Those are they who have gone utterly astray. From anyone of those who have disbelieved, and die while they are disbelievers, there shall not be accepted even an earthful of gold, though he offer it in ransom. For those there shall be a grievous punishment, and they shall have no helper.

(3.86-92)

It is obvious from these verses that no punishment is to be inflicted by one man on another for apostasy. The words 'thereunder shall they abide' clearly refer to the life hereafter. By no stretch of imagination can any sane person interpret the words 'curse of Allah' to be a licence to murder anyone whom he considers to be an apostate. No capital punishment is mentioned. If it had, according to the strict requirements of the law, the punishment would have been clearly defined, as in the case of all other *hodud* (punishments specifically prescribed in the Holy Quran). On the contrary, the Holy Quran mentions the possibility of repentance by such persons and subsequent forgiveness by God. How can anyone repent and atone for his sins in this world if he has been killed?

The advocates of capital punishment for apostasy need to consider how, if their tradition is presumed to be accurate, the clear contradiction between it and the Holy Quran is to be resolved. In particular, they should reconsider their stance in view of the verses quoted above and re-examine those with an impartial mind. How could anyone accredit greater weight to such a dubious tradition than to these manifestly clear dictates of the Holy Quran:

If thy Lord had enforced His Will, surely all those on the earth would have believed without exception. Will thou than take it upon thyself to force people to become believers? Except by Allah's leave no one can believe and He will afflict with His wrath those who will not use their understanding. (10.100-1)

When God Himself does not force people to believe, who are we to raise the sword to force belief or to set Maududian mouse-traps? The problem with the advocates of capital punishment for apostasy is that they invariably accept literally traditions compiled hundreds of years after the Holy Prophet[sa] which obviously contradict the teachings contained in the Holy Quran.

Conflicts with the practice of the Holy Prophet[sa]

Our second source of law is the conduct and personal example of the Holy Prophet[sa]. We have already demonstrated the hollowness of the claim that anyone has ever been executed for the crime of apostasy.

After all, what was the stand of the Holy Prophet[sa] against the Meccans? It was that he should be allowed to profess and proclaim the message of God in peace. The Meccans did not grant him this freedom and punished those who began to believe in him. As far as the Meccans were concerned, those who believed in the message of Muhammad[sa] were the apostates, having recanted their faith of idol worship.

The Holy Prophet[sa] spent his entire life fighting in defence of the fundamental human rights that everybody should be free to choose his religion, no one should change another person's religion by force, and everybody has a right to change his own religion, whatever that religion is.

In fact, this has been the true meaning of 'Holy War', waged by all messengers of God against their opponents throughout the history of religion. The Holy Quran has repeatedly mentioned this with reference to earlier prophets of God (see 2.5; 6.113; 21.42; 25.32; 36.8, 31; 43.8). To name but a few, these are Abraham[as] (6.75-9; 19.47; 21.53, 59, 61, 69 -70; 37.89-91, 98); Elias[as] (37.126-7); Lot[as] (26.166-8; 27.57;15.71); Noah[as] (7.60; 10.72; 11.26-7; 26.117; 71.2-21); Moses[as] (7.105-6, 124-7; 10.76-9; 17.102-3; 20.44-5; 50-3; 26.19-34); and Jesus[as] (3.52-6; 5.118; 19.37; 43.65). What was their struggle about? It was simply a response to the claim of the opponents of the prophets[as] that they had no right to change the faith of their contemporaries. In fact everybody has a right to choose his faith and as long as the message of peace and love is spread by peaceful means, no one has the right to prevent this by force. The obstinate response of the opponents to this most logical and humane stance was that they positively rejected the prophets' position and stuck to their claim that the prophets had no right to change the faith of their people. If they did not desist from this course, the prophets were to be ready to accept the penalty for apostasy which was (in the opponents' opinion) no other than death or exile.

The Holy Prophet's[sa] struggle with his opponents was consistent with the practice of all prophets of the past. How can any sane person deny the lifetime mission of the Holy Prophet[sa] and challenge his firm stance on this fundamental principle? The Holy Quran, the practice of the Holy Prophet[sa], and the other traditions provide ample contradiction to the tradition in question. One cannot over-emphasise the utter unreliability of this tradition.

Reliability of the sources and narrators
Prima facie, the tradition refuted here has been authenticated by the reputable compilers Bukhari, Tirmidhi, Abu Daud, Al-Nisai and Ibn Majah; it is included in five out of the six generally accepted compilations of *hadith*. But there ends its claim to authenticity.

For a tradition to be declared authentic it is not enough for it to be found in an authentic compilation. There are other established measures which are applied to every tradition. The most important among these measures is the examination in depth and detail of the reputation and character of the narrators forming the links in the chain of narrators.

There are scholars who have devoted their whole lifetime to such studies and, thanks to their most painstaking and thorough investigations, we are today in a position to examine every link of the chain of narrators in any compilation. Let us turn our attention to the tradition under consideration. This *hadith* falls into the category of *ahad gharib* (i.e., a tradition in which there is only one chain of narrators connected to the same single source) because all the five books of *hadith* derive their chain of narrators from Ikramah as their ultimate source.

The late Maulana Abdul Hayy of Lucknow specifically refers to Ikramah, pointing out that merely because Bukhari had included him in his compilation, others followed suit without carrying out independent research.[15]

A tradition may be authentic and reliable even if it is quoted through a single chain of narrators. However, it cannot be regarded as being as reliable as traditions which have more than one chain of reliable narrators. Such traditions are not permitted to influence edicts regarding the rights, liabilities and penalties; in particular, extra caution is required in relation to *hodud*. *Hodud* is a term strictly applicable to punishments specifically prescribed in the Holy Quran. The exponents of death as the penalty for apostasy consider their view to be based on Quranic injunctions falling within the category of *hodud*. In fact, we have disproved this claim earlier.

It is important to bear in mind that the tradition under discussion is a tradition quoted by a single chain of narrators and has no jurisprudence even if it is considered to be correct by some. In this context, it is essential to learn more about Ikramah and his reputation.

Ikramah

Ikramah[16] was a slave of Ibn Abbas, and also his pupil - a very indifferent pupil, for that matter, and a back-bencher of the first order. He confirms this himself by saying that Ibn Abbas was so infuriated with his lack of interest in his studies and by his truancy that he would bind his hand and foot to compel him to remain present during his sermons.[17]

He was an opponent of Hazrat Ali, the fourth caliph of Islam, and was inclined towards the Khawarij in particular at the time when differences between Hazrat Ali and Ibn Abbas began to emerge. Later, during the Abbaside period, (the Abbasides, it should be borne in mind, were extremely antagonistic to all those who were in any way allied to Hazrat Ali's progeny because of political apprehensions), Ikramah acquired great renown and respect as a versatile scholar, obviously because of his hostility towards Hazrat Ali and links with the Khawarij.[18]

Dhahbi states that because Ikramah was a Kharijite, his traditions were unreliable and dubious. An expert on the punishment for apostasy, Imam Ali b. Al-Medaini, is of the same opinion. Yahya b. Bekir used to say that the Kharijites of Egypt, Algiers and Morocco were strongly allied to Ikramah.

It has generally been observed that the traditions of capital punishment for apostasy emanate mainly from incidents in Basra, Kufa and Yemen. The people of the Hejaz (Mecca and Medina) were totally unfamiliar with them. One cannot shut one's eyes to the fact that the tradition from Ikramah under discussion is known as an Iraqi tradition. Let us recall the famous Meccan Imam, Taus b. Kaisan, who used to say that Iraqi traditions were generally doubtful.[19]

That is not all. A great scholar, Yahya b. Saeed Al-Ansari, has strongly censured Ikramah for his unreliability in general and has gone to the extent of calling him a *kadhab*,[20] that is to say an extreme liar of the first water.

Abdullah b. Al-Harith quotes a very interesting incident which he witnessed himself when he visited Ali b. Abdullah b. Abbas. He was deeply shocked and dismayed to find Ikramah bound to a post outside the door of Ali b. Abdullah b. Abbas. He expresseed his shock at this cruelty by asking Ali b. Abdullah b. Abbas if he had no fear of God in him. What he obviously meant was that Ikramah, with all his renown of piety and so on, did not deserve such a base and cruel treatment at the hands of his late master's own son. In response to this, Ali b. Abdullah b. Abbas justified his act by pointing out that Ikramah had the audacity to attribute false things to his late father, Ibn Abbas.[21] What better judge of the character of Ikramah could there be than Ali b. Abdullah b. Abbas? No wonder, therefore, that Imam Malik b. Anas (95-179 AH), the pioneer compiler of *hadith* and an Imam of jurisprudence held in the highest repute throughout the Muslim world, held that the traditions narrated by Ikramah were unreliable.[22]

The following scholars of great repute have declared that Ikramah had a strong disposition towards exaggeration: Imam Yayha b. Saeed Al-Ansari, Ali b. Abdullah b. Abbas and Ata b. Abi Rabae.[23]

This, then, is the man who we are dealing with and on whose sole authority the matter of the lives of all those people who change their faith is left hanging till the end of time.

Ibn Abbas

Whenever the name of Ibn Abbas[24] appears at the head of a chain of narrators, the vast majority of Muslim scholars is overawed. They forget the fact that because of his name and reputation concocters of false traditions tended to trace their fabricated chain of narrators back to him. Therefore, all traditions beginning with the name of Ibn Abbas must be properly judged and examined.

Moreover, even if Ibn Abbas is honestly reported by a narrator, the possiblity of human error on Ikramah's part regarding what Ibn Abbas might have said cannot be ruled out. The following would be a good illustration of the case in point:

> Ibn Abbas says that Umar used to say that the Holy Prophet[sa] said that crying over the dead brought chastisement to the dead. Ibn Abbas further said that after Umar died, he related this tradition to Ayesha who said, 'God forgive Umar!' By God, the Holy Prophet[sa] said nothing of the

kind. He only said that if the descendants of a disbeliever cried over his dead body, their action tended to augment his punishment, and by way of argument, Ayesha also said, 'Sufficient for us is the saying of the Quran: "Verily no soul can bear the burden of another."'[25]

If a man of Hazrat Umar's stature and integrity can misunderstand the Holy Prophet[sa], however rarely it might have happened, how much more is there danger of ordinary narrators misunderstanding the reports of Ibn Abbas?

With such wide possibilities for the miscarriage of the message of the Holy Prophet of Islam[sa], how can a sane person rely entirely on the evidence of this *hadith* and draw conclusions of far-reaching import regarding matters of life and death and fundamental human rights?

It is likely that Ikramah concocted this tradition, attributing it to Ibn Abbas, as it was his wont to do, according to Ali b. Ibn Abbas.

Other internal criteria

When we examine the subject matter of the tradition under consideration, we find the contents to be erroneous in several ways.

a) A person of Hazrat Ali's stature is presumed to be unaware of the fact that Islam categorically prohibits a person to be punished by fire.

b) The words 'slay whosoever changes his faith' are so general that they can be interpreted in many ways. They can apply to men, women and children, whereas according to Imam Abu Hanifa and some other schools of jurisprudence, an apostate woman can never be slain.

c) The Arabic word *deen* (religion) used in this tradition is a general word meaning any religion, not Islam specifically. Even the faith of idolaters is referred to as *deen*. (Sura Al-Kafiroon)

In the light of the general nature of the language used, how can one restrict the application of this tradition to a Muslim who renounces his faith? In strict legal terms, according to this tradition anyone who changes his religion, whatever that religion is, would have to be put to death. It would mean slaying the Jew who became a Christian, slaying the Christian who became a Muslim, and slaying the pagan who adopted any new faith. 'Whosoever' also transcends the geographical boundaries of Muslim states, implying that anywhere in the world, anyone who changes his faith - be he an aborigine of Australia, a pygmy of Africa or an indian of South America - must be slain forthwith the moment he renounces his previous faith and accepts another one.

Islam lays a great deal of emphasis on proselytizing, so that it is binding upon every Muslim to become a preacher in the path of Allah. How ironical it is therefore that many renowned Muslim scholars today negate the very spirit of Islamic *jihad* by audaciously sticking to the narrow-minded view that Islam dictates that whosoever changes his faith, meaning in this context Islam, must be put to death forthwith. What about those of other faiths? Islam declares it to be an obligation upon Muslims to stand committed to the noble goal of constantly endeavouring to change the faith of all non-Muslims around them by peaceful means. This task is so important and demanding that every Muslim is instructed to stick to the endeavour till his last breath.

The Holy Quran states:

Call unto the way of thy Lord with wisdom and goodly exhortation, and reason with them on the basis of that which is best. Thy Lord knows best those who have strayed away from His way; and He knows best those who are rightly guided. (16.126)

The advocates of the bigoted inhumane doctrine of death upon apostasy never visualise its effect on international and interreligious human relationships. Why can they not see that according to their view of Islam, adherents of all religions have a fundamental right to change their faith but not so the Muslims, and that Islam has the prerogative of converting others but all adherents of different faiths are deprived of any right to convert Muslims to their faith? What a sorry picture of Islamic justice this presents!

To conclude, apostasy is the clear repudiation of a faith by a person who formerly held it. Doctrinal differences, however grave, cannot be deemed to be apostasy. The punishment for apostasy lies in the hand of God Almighty, against whom the offence has been committed. Apostasy which is not aggravated by some other crime is not punishable in this world. This is the teaching of God. This was the teaching of the Holy Prophet[sa]. This is the view confirmed by Hanafi jurists,[26] *Fateh al-Kadeer*,[27] Chalpi,[28] Hafiz ibn Qayyam, Ibrahim Nakhai, Sufyan Thauri and many others. The Maududian claim of consensus, concerning the tradition they hold to be true, is a mere fiction.

CHAPTER 8

MERCY FOR THE UNIVERSE

They were clever enough to realise that a Musalman's feelings are never more easily aroused than over a real or fancied insult to the Holy Prophet. They, therefore, began to proclaim that their activites were meant to preserve the *nubuwwat* [prophethood] of the Holy Prophet and to repel attacks on his *namus* [honour]. . . . The trick succeeded and they began to attract large audiences to their meetings. Since some of the Ahrar speakers are experts in the choice of words and expression and the use of similes and metaphors and can intersperse their speeches with flashes of humour of however low an order, they soon began gaining in popularity.

Justice Mr Munir[1]

Disparaging a prophet of God is as old as the prophethood itself. Even Muhammad[sa] could not escape it. He was mocked, not only during the Meccan period of his life, but also in Medina where he had the authority to punish. The Jews of Medina had sharp tongues and a sick sense of humour, and did not miss an opportunity of ridiculing the Prophet[sa].

After the Hijrah, the Quraish of Mecca joined forces with these Jews to stop the progress of Islam. The hypocrites were already there, starting work as fifth columnists. Apart from intrigue and war, they also employed the communications network for anti-Muslim propaganda. The propagandist poets, whom Maxime Rodinson has described as 'the journalists of the time' and Carmichael as kindlers of battle,[2] accused the Medinite Muslims of dishonouring themselves by submitting to an outsider. Abu Afak taunted the children of Qayla (the Aws and the Khazraj):

I have lived a long time, but I have never seen
Either a house or gathering of People
More loyal and faithful to
Its allies, when they call on it,
Than that of the children of Qayla

(the Aws and the Khazraj) as a whole.
The mountains will crumble before they submit
Yet here is a rider come among them who had divided them.
(He says) 'This is permitted; this is forbidden'
To all kinds of things.
But if you had believed in power
And in might, why did you not follow a *tubba*?[3]

Abu 'Afak in effect was saying, 'The *tubba* was, after all, a south Arabian king of great reputation, yet you resisted him. Now what has happened to you that you have accepted the claims of a Meccan refugee?' Meanwhile, Kab was elected chief of the Jews, replacing Malik b. al-Sayf[4] who also lamented the loss of Quraish at Badr.[5] In an elegy he said:

Drive out that fool of yours that you may be safe
From talk that has no sense!
Do you taunt me because I shed tears
For people who loved me sincerely?
As long as I live I shall weep and remember
The merits of people whose glory is the houses of Mecca.[6]

Obviously, the main purpose of this vulgar and abusive campaign was to sow the seeds of dissention between the Ansar and the Muhajirs on the one hand and between the Aws and the Khazraj on the other. The campaign seemed to pay off when a Jew from the Banu Qaynuqa, Shas b. Qays, ordered a Jewish youth to recite some poems composed at the battle of Buath. They were recited to a mixed gathering of Muslims, comprising the Aws and the Khazraj. Eventually, both sides got worked up and challenged each other, saying: 'If you wish we will do the same thing again.' They both replied: 'We will! Your meeting place is outside - that being the volcanic tract. To arms! To arms!'[7] As soon as the Holy Prophet[sa] heard the news he hurried to the spot with the Emigrants and addressed the men of the Aws and the Khazraj:

O Muslims! Remember God, remember God. Will you act like pagans while I am with you? After God has guided you to Islam and honoured you and saved you from paganism? After he has delivered you from unbelief and made you friends by so doing?[8]

The following verses of the Quran were revealed on the occasion:[10]

O ye who believe ... if you obey any of those who have been given the Book, they will turn you again into disbelievers after you have believed. When you are the people to whom the signs of Allah are given and among whom the Messenger of Allah is present, how can you disbelieve? He who holds fast to Allah is indeed guided to the right path.

> O ye who believe, be mindful of your duty to Allah in all respects,
> every moment of your lives, so that whenever death overtakes you, it will
> find you in a state of complete submission to Him. All of you, take hold
> of Allah's rope which He gave you when you hated each other. He united
> your hearts in love so that by His grace you became brethren.
>
> (3:103, 104)

This was the atmosphere of unrest in Medina when the Prophet[sa] decided to stop the poet's propaganda campaign and ask for volunteers to execute them. It was clear they had become a grave danger to peace. To say that they were killed because they reviled and insulted the Prophet[sa] is to twist historical fact. To use these executions as a precedent for the execution of those who defame the Prophet[sa] is either deliberate dishonesty or sheer historical ignorance. Defaming the Prophet[sa], known technically as *sabb*, is neither a *hadd* offence according to the Quran nor a capital offence according to the *Sunnah*. In fact it is not punishable at all, unless there are contributing circumstances. Its punishment, like that of apostasy, is in the hands of Allah alone. The Quran uses goodwill to uphold the honour of Allah and his prophets, not the sword. The Quran says:

> Revile not those to whom they pray besides Allah, lest they wrongfully
> revile Allah through ignorance. Thus unto every nation have We made
> their deed seem fair. Then unto their Lord is their return, and He will tell
> them what they used to do. (6.109)

Respect, honour, love and esteem for someone come from the heart. Force can shut mouths, create terror and result in disrespect and irreverence. This is why the Quran takes a positive view in matters of the heart.

As regards respect for the Holy Prophet[sa], the Quran says:

> Lo! Allah and His angels shower blessings on the Prophet. O ye who
> believe! Ask blessings on him and honour him with a worthy salutation.
> Lo! Those who malign Allah and His Messenger Allah hath cursed them
> in this world and in the next and hath prepared for them the doom of the
> disdained. And those who malign believing men and women undeserv-
> edly, they bear the guilt of slander and manifest sin. (33:5-59)

The Quran is very clear about *sabb*. It asks Muslims not to scorn even the false gods of unbelievers and it does not lay down any punishment for those who show disrespect to the Prophet[sa] - for them, God has prepared the 'doom of the disdained'.

And how did the Excellent Exampler[sa] treat those who reviled him? Let us return to the leader of the *munafiqun*, Abdullah b. Ubayy. After the battle of Al-Mustaliq (6AH/AD737), while the Holy Prophet[sa] was staying by the watering-place of Al-Muraysi, an unpleasant dispute took place between the Muhajirs and Ansar. A hired servant of Umar, Jahjah b. Masud, and Sinan b. Wabar al-Juhani, an ally of Ansar, began fighting. According to Ibn Ishaq:

> The Juhani called out: 'Men of Al-Ansar!' and Jahjah called out 'Men of the Muhajirun!' Abdullah b. Ubayy b. Salul was enraged. With him were some of his people, including Zayd b. Arqam, a young boy. He said: 'Have they actually done this? They dispute our priority, they outnumber us in our country. Nothing is more apt for us and the vagabonds of Quraish than the ancient saying, "Feed a dog and it will devour you." By Allah, when we return to Medina the most honourable will drive out the meanest.' Then he went to his people and said: 'This is what you have done to yourselves. You have let them occupy your country and you have divided your property among them. Had you only kept your property from them they would have gone elsewhere.' Zayd b. Arqam heard this and, when he had disposed of his enemies, went and told the Prophet[sa]. Umar, who was with him, said: 'Tell Abbad b. Bishr to go and kill him.' The Prophet[sa] answered: 'What if men should say Muhammad kills his own Companions? No, but give orders to set off.'[10]

The Holy Prophet[sa] was, of course, greatly upset. The tribal appeal of Juhani to Ansar and Jahjah's call to 'the men of Mahajirun' reminded him of the Day of Buath and the war of Basus, which lasted forty years. Had Abdullah b. Ubayy succeeded the Ansar, the Muhajirs would have gone back to their tribal wars. The message of Islamic unity, which changed these disunited tribes into a mighty Arab nation, would have been lost forever. The Holy Prophet[sa] was so upset that he gave orders to move, although, as Ibn Ishaq reports, 'This was at a time when the Prophet[sa] was not used to travelling.'[11] Referring to this incident, the Quran says:

> They [the Munafiqun] say: 'When we return to Medina the one most honourable shall surely drive out the meanest.' True honour belongs to Allah, to His Messenger and believers; but the hypocrites know it not. (63.9)

When Abdullah, son of Abdullah b. Ubayy, heard of this affair, he went to the Prophet[sa] and said:

> I have heard that you want to kill Abdullah b. Ubayy for what you heard about him. If you must, order me to do it and I will bring his head, for Al-Khazraj know they have no man more dutiful to his father than I. I am afraid that if you order someone else to kill him, I could not bear to see his executioner walking around and might kill him. I would therefore be killing a believer for an unbeliever and I would certainly be damned.' The

Prophet[sa] said: 'No, but let us deal kindly with him and make much of his companionship while he is with us.'[12]

Muslim rulers, who understood why the Holy Prophet[sa] treated Abdullah b. Ubayy and other hypocrites and Jews as he did, have been extremely reluctant to create false martyrs in the process of protecting the honour of the Prophet[sa] (Namus-i-Rasul). In Cordova, between 850 and 859, a group of Christian zealots was formed under the leadership of Eulogius. The members of this group were determined to denounce the Holy Prophet[sa] publicly and to accept martyrdom. The *qadis* of Cordova, however, refused to oblige them and jailed them instead. Will Durant reports one such incident:

> Isaac, a Cardovan monk, went to the *qadi* and professed a desire for conversion; but when the judge, well pleased, began to expound Mohammedanism, the monk interrupted him: 'Your Prophet', he said, 'has lied and deceived you. May he be cursed, who has dragged so many wretches with him down to hell!' The *qadi* reproved him and asked had he been drinking? The monk replied: 'I am in my right mind. Condemn me to death.' The *qadi* had him imprisoned, but asked permission of Abd-ur Rahman II to dismiss him as insane.[13]

Shaykhul Islam Ebussuud Efendi, chief mufti of the Ottoman Empire during the reign of the Sultan Suleyman the Magnificent, allowed the death penalty, but only for habitual and public defamers of the Holy Prophet[sa]. Shaykhul Islam went out of his way to insist that execution should not be ordered lightly. He clearly wished to avoid frivolous and malicious prosecutions and laid down that an offender could not be treated as habitual 'merely on the word of one or two persons'. The habitual character of the offender had to be proved to the authorities by impartial (*begharaz*) Muslims, who had no axe to grind. But there was an important rider to this which showed that though Shaykhul Islam Ebussuud issued a *fatwa* without any Quranic or *hadith* authority, he knew the punishment of *sabb* was Allah's alone. The *fatwa* was issued, probably under political pressure, because he nullified its entire effect by stating that unbelievers were not held guilty for declaring 'that which constitutes their disbelief': that is, for rejecting Muhammad's[sa] prophetic mission.

The quality of a Muslim's faith and the measure of respect he holds for the Prophet[sa] cannot be legally defined. Conversely, an unbeliever can neither be forced to embrace Islam nor to honour its Prophet[sa] at gun-point. This is why God has prescribed no punishment for *irtidad* or *sabb* in this world. Despite the disparaging words uttered by Abdullah b.

Ubayy at the watering-hole of Al-Muraysi, the Holy Prophet[sa] did not punish him.

The punishment of these two offences is easily exploited by politically orientated *ulema* who would debase religious causes by using them for materialist purposes and exploit religious belief for their own ends.[14]

At the moment, Deobandi/Ahli *hadith ulema* are accusing the Ahmadis of disparaging the Prophet[sa]. Little do they realise that in doing so they have created the means of their own destruction. In comparison with mainstream Sunnis, who constitute the majority of Muslims in the subcontinent,[15] Turkey, and many other Muslim countries, the Deobandis/Ahli *hadith* and the followers of the Najdi reformer Abdul Wahhab are in a minority throughout the Muslim world (except in Nejd). They are accused of belittling the Prophet[sa]. The Deobandi/Wahhabi *ulema* consider the mainstream Sunnis to be *kafir* for attributing to the Prophet[sa] qualities which, to say the least, are polytheist. For instance, they say that his body did not cast a shadow because he was filled with light. When *Meauud-i-Sherif*, popularised by the Turkish poet Suleyman Chelebi of Busra (1410), is concluded with *ya Nabi Salam Alaika* (peace be with you), the Prophet's[sa] soul is present at the event, and, therefore, everyone attending should stand to show respect. In the same manner, praying at his tomb, kissing the grillework surrounding it and many other such beliefs and practices of the Sunnis/Brelvis are *shirk* according to Deobandis. The Wahhabis, having demolished the historical graveyard of *Jannat ul- Baqi*, wished to destroy even the dome of the Prophet's[sa] mosque and were prevented from doing so only by the strong reaction in the Muslim world. For these acts of destruction of graves, tombs and domes, Sunnis all over the world accuse the Wahhabis of denigrating and belittling the Holy Prophet[sa]. The Brelvis consider that it was the Deoband scholars Maulana Muhammad Qasim Nanautwi and Maulana Ashraf Ali Thanwi, who did not believe in *Khatm-i-nubuwatt*. In a booklet, *Deobandi Maulwiyon ka Iman*, Maulana Abdul Mustafa Abu Yahya Muhammad Muinuddin Shafi 'i Qadri Rizvi Thanwi writes:

> O Muslims! Look how this accursed, unholy, satanic assertion has destroyed the very basis of *Khatm-i-nubuwatt* . . . . See that Maulwi Qasim Nanautwi does not believe in *Khatm-i-nubuwatt*, while Maulwi Rashid Ahmad, Maulwi Khalil Ahmad and other Wahhabi *ulema* have declared those who reject *Khatm-i-nubuwatt* as *kafir*.[16]

Brelvi-Deobandi polemics - all in the name of protecting the Holy Prophet[sa], the very paragon of modesty - have reached such vulgarity that even the mildest examples are offensive. Shourish Kashmiri, a supporter of the Deobandi school, said in his pamphlet '*Kafir saz Mulla*' that anyone who declares the great leader of Deoband as *kafir* (unbeliever) is a liar. In the same pamphlet he said that the Brelvi/*ulema* sell religion and the Sharia of the Prophet[sa] to make a living, that they are the born slaves of Lord Clive's household, the enemies of the Muslim League and Qaid-i-Azam Jinnah. In another pamphlet, he said that these people were even lower than a brick in Maulana Husain Ahmad's and Syed Ataullah Shah Bukhari's lavatory.[16] The Brelvi reply to these abusive charges was tasteless. They said that the man slandering them and the Holy Prophet[sa] had spent his life wandering the red-light districts. 'The man who called Nehru a prophet is now accusing us of selling the Shari'a of the Prophet[sa]', they cried. 'Why shouldn't Muhammad Qasim Nanautwi be called a *kafir* and how can we accept Ashraf Ali Thanwi as a Muslim? Aren't they the men who said the door of prophethood was open? Aren't they the pathfinders of the Qadiyanis? Who has taught you how to denigrate Mustafa? Who has taught you unbelief? You have taken your clothes off, have you no sense of decency or modesty? You have created disorder under the name of *khatm-i-nubuwwat* and spread mischief under the name of peace. You are collecting money under the name of *nubuwwat* and begging under the name of the Prophet[sa].'

Another poet, Sayyad Muhammad Tanha, said:
How can you appreciate the high status of Ahmad Raza?
Go and smell the stinking underpants of Hindus.
Gold is your prophet, gold is your God
You belong to the party of those who show you gold
You have spent all your life with *Kufr*
How can you, a Khatri Hindu by caste, join Islam?
O Nimrod, how can you glorify Allah?
Your place is with Hindus, go there and praise
    there the name of Hari, Hari.[18]

Compare the language, the style and the contents of this Barelvi attack on Deobandi *ulema* with the tirade of Deobandi scholars against Ahmadis:

1. Ahmadis deny *khatm-i-nubuwwat*;
2. Ahmadis denigrate the Holy Prophet[sa];
3. Ahmadis created British imperialism in India;
4. Ahmadis opposed the creation of Pakistan;
5. Ahmadis are opposed to *jihad*;
6. Ahmadis associate with non-Muslims;
7. Ahmadiyat is a racket in religion's name.

Both the Ahli-Sunnat wal Jamaat (Brelvi) and Deobandi *ulema* accuse each other of disparaging the Holy Prophet[sa]. As we saw earlier, the Jamaati Islami described the Ahl-i Quran as being worse than the Ahmadis. But the Shias have not been spared either - they have been accused of degrading the status of the Holy Prophet[sa] by claiming that Ali shared the prophethood with him.

The Canadian scholar, Wilfred Cantwell Smith, who visited the subcontinent and closely observed the Muslim society of India and Pakistan, has accused Muslims of 'a fanaticism of blazing vehemence'. In his book, *Islam in Modern India*, he says:

> Muslims will allow attacks on Allah: there are atheists and atheistic publications and rationalistic societies, but to disparage Muhammad will provoke from even the most liberal sections of the community a fanaticism of blazing vehemence.[19]

This is an incorrect assessment of Muslim temperament. Prof. Cantwell Smith has generalised. Actually, it is the Mullahs and the politically-orientated leadership which recognised: 'that the feelings of a Musulman are never more easily aroused and his indignation awakened than over a real or fancied insult to the Holy Prophet.'[20]

No doubt the rich and the poor, the intellectuals, the uneducated, the pious and impious have always been united in the love of the Prophet[sa] and considered *fana fir-rasul* (annihilation in the name of the Prophet[sa]) to be the peak of religious experience. But no Muslim is unmindful that the Holy Prophet's[sa] highest experience was the *miraj*, when he, surrounded by clouds of angels, soared high into the Divine Presence, where even the angel Gabriel has no access. The power-hungry Muslim leadership forgets that the exhortation 'Muhammad[sa] is the Messenger of God' is only the second part of the confession of the Muslim faith. The first is: 'There is no God but Allah.'

There is no way to measure love or respect. Lovers and mystics wrote *diwans* after *diwans* and finally devoted their lives to trying to express feelings no language could really convey. The mullahs can scan the poem of love, but cannot understand it. It is no mere accident that the founder of the Ahmadiyyah Movement in Islam was named Ghulam Ahmad[as]. What an honour! What a status! What a glory! In the following three couplets he answers those who accuse him of disparaging the Holy Prophet[sa] and critics, like Cantwell Smith, who accuse Muslims of being negligent of Allah's honour:

After the love of Allah it is Muhammad's love
  which has captivated my heart;
If this love be *kufr*, by God I am a great *kafir*.[21]
My Love! My Benefactor! Let my life be sacrificed in Thy way,
For when hath Thou shown indifference in Thy goodness to this slave?[22]
If it be the custom that claimants of
Thy love be beheaded at Thy threshold,
Then let it be known I am the first to claim that reward.[23]

The founder[as] of the Ahmadiyyah Movement in Islam has clearly and honestly declared his faith in the supreme authority of the Holy Prophet[sa] as the *Khatam-un-nabiyyin*. He said:

> The basis of our religion and the essence of our belief is that there is no God but Allah and Muhammad is His Prophet. The faith that we follow in this earthly life and the faith in which, by the grace of God, we shall depart from this transitory abode, is that of our Lord and great Master, Muhammad - may peace and blessings of Allah be upon him. And it is *Khatam-un-nabiyyin*, nabuwwat, prophethood are the great blessings, leading man straight to God and it has reached that state of completion to which nothing can be added.[24]

And, again:

> A superior status, comprising all that is good, belongs to our Lord and Master, Seal of the Prophets, Muhammad Mustafa[sa]. It is unique to him, it is unapproachable.[25]

The writer of the four quotations given above, Mirza Ghulam Ahmad[as], and his followers have been declared non-Muslims by Muslims described by Sir Muhammad Iqbal (1875-1938) in the following stanzas of a long Urdu poem:

> Hands are impotent and nerveless,
> hearts unfaithful and infidel,
>
> The Community a heartbreak to
> their Prophet and a shame;
>
> Gone are the idol-breakers, in their
> places idol-makers dwell;
>
> Abraham their father was: the
> children merit Azar's name.[26]
>
> New and strange the band of drinkers,
> and their wine is strange and new,

Murder in the Name of Allah

A new shrine to house their Kaaba,
new and strange the idols too.

Very heavy on your spirits weighs the
charge of morning's prayer;

How much more would you prefer sleeping, than
rising up to worship me.

Ramadan is too oppressive for you
tempers free to bear;

Tell me now, do you consider *that* the
law of loyalty?

Nations come to birth by faith; let
faith expire, and nations die

So, when gravitation ceases, the
throngéd stars asunder fly.

Why, you are a people utterly bereft
of every art;

No other nation in the world so lightly
spurns its native place;

You are like a barn where lightnings
nestle, and will not depart;

You would sell your fathers' graveyards,
And say that such a thing was right;

Making profit out of tombstones has
secured you such renown -

Why not set up shop in idols, if you
chance to hunt some down?

Loud the cry goes up 'The Muslims?
They are vanished, lost to view',

We re-echo, 'Are true Muslims to be
found in any place?'

Christian is your mode of living, and
your culture is Hindu;

Why, such Muslims to the Jews would
be a shame and a disgrace.

Sure enough, you have your Syeds,
Mirzas, Afghans, all the rest;

But can you claim that you are Muslims
if the truth must be confessed?[27]

Having claimed that the Muslims of the day would shame even Jews, and that they would even sell their ancestors' tombstones, the 'poet, philosopher, political thinker and altogether most eminent figure in Indian Islam of the twentieth century'[28] decided to distinguish between Muslims and Ahmadis. So in 1936 he wrote in an open letter to Pandit Jawaharlal Nehru, the leader of the predominantly Hindu Indian National Congress and, later, first prime minister of India, demanding that Ahmadis should be declared a non-Muslim minority. In the constitution of secular India the demand was, of course, ignored. But for the *ulema* of Deoband it was a matter of life and death. Hindus have occupied Babari Masjid in Ayodhya and converted it under police protection into the Ram Janma Bhoomi temple. Another section of Hindus demand the conversion of Benares and Kashi mosques into temples. Most Hindus are agitating for the abolition of Muslim personal law.

This is what becomes of people who reject prophets of God and men of peace. They stand disunited and bereft of the blessings of the peace they sought to disturb. They breed violence and terrorism.

CHAPTER 9

ISLAMIC TERRORISM?

What is 'Islamic' terrorism, I wonder? Islam is as closely related to terrorism as light is to darkness or life is to death or peace is to war. They do come into contact with each other, of course, but from directions diametrically opposed. They are found grappling with each other but never walking hand in hand happily together.

However, one cannot deny that on many occasions some Muslims are found involved in terrorist activities either on behalf of a group or on behalf of a country with a predominately Muslim population.

Are there not equally, other groups involved in terrorism and subversion throughout the world? Would it be fitting to label all brands of terrorism by using the same principle which gave birth to the term 'Islamic terrorism' creating a list of Sikh terrorism, Hindu terrorism, Christian terrorism, Jewish terrorism, atheist terrorism, Buddhist terrorism, Animist terrorism and pagan terrorism?

It is not easy to close one's eyes to various brands of terrorism which unfortunately flourish all over the world; in fact, it is impossible for an observer not to be aware of the persecution, bloodshed and murder, often in the name of some purported ideal or noble cause. Terrorism is a global problem and needs to be studied in its larger perspective. Unless we understand the forces behind the violence, we shall not be able to understand why some Muslim groups and states are turning to terrorism to achieve certain objectives.

I am fully convinced that almost every form of communal violence witnessed in the world today, wherever that is and whatever cloak it wears, is essentially political in nature. Religion is not the exploiter; it is itself exploited by internal or external political interests.

For instance, we find terrorism generated by racialism - but that, in the final analysis, is essentially political in nature. There are other small expressions of terrorism born out of rebellion and hatred against prevailing social systems and cultures. These are generally regarded as acts of madmen and anarchists. There is a special kind of terrorism which is related to the Mafia's struggle for supremacy; this terrorism is directed by certain factions against other factions within the Mafia. Obviously, this terrorism is really a power struggle and therefore political.

When we examine so-called 'Islamic terrorism', we discover political forces working behind an Islamic facade. More often than not, the real manipulators and exploiters are not even Muslims themselves. Let us turn to some particular illustrations of terrorism in order to diagnose the underlying maladies. We shall begin with Iran and see how Khomeinism came to be born.

It is common knowledge that in the days of the Shah there was great prosperity. The highly ambitious industrial and economic development plans augered a bright future for the country. But can man live by bread alone? As far as Iranians under the despotic rule of the Shah were concerned, the answer was an emphatic 'No'. They wanted to have a responsible share in the running of affairs in their own country. They could no longer just be satisfied with full stomachs . Their hunger for self-respect and dignity and their craving for freedom and liberation from a highly regimented system of oppression made them more and more restive and volatile. This situation was ripe for a violent and bloody revolution.

If the nature of this imminent revolution had not been essentially Islamic, it would have been a communist revolution and could have been even bloodier and more extreme. The turmoil which was to shake Iran from north to south and east to west was a natural and inevitable consequence of a long political oppression and negation of fundamental human rights and liberties, and also of subversion and exploitation by a great Western foreign power. Iran was aware of the fact that the despotic regime of the Shah was fully backed, supported and sanctioned by the government of the United States of America. The people's hatred and urge for revenge did not stop at the toppling of the Shah's regime and the destruction of all internal forces which in one way or another had been responsible for the maintenance of the monarchy.

The consciousness of American support had brought out in the Shah the very worst of his despotic tendencies. He had been held in awe to begin with, but gradually awe gave way to terror. The fear of revolt stiffened his attitude even more with the passage of time. Gradually a police state of the worst type came to be born in Iran. With the passage of time Iranians became aware that the police state was fully and un-equivocally supported by the government of the USA. The Shah played the part of a mere puppet whose strings were tied to the subtle, manipulating fingers of USA. This, as has been mentioned above, led to a situation ripe for revolution motivated by a consuming fire of hatred.

The situation was capitalised upon by Ayatollah Khomeini. The ideology which he propounded to give colour and complexion to his revolution was Shia Islam. But was it really a love of Shia Islam which generated hatred against the USA, or was the name of Islam a mere facade to hide the underlying motives? Had Khomeini not raised the banner of Islam, would there not have been a revolution in some other name? Is it not a fact that had Khomeini not exploited the situation and given it an Islamic colour and complexion, the same situation of hatred could have been equally well exploited by a non-religious philosophy such as nationalism or scientific socialism?

In fact Khomeini outpaced forces which were coming fast at his heels and which, given time, might have overtaken him and all he stood for. That is why the situation in Iran became extremely complicated and confused. The basic urge of the revolution was not against communism or any leftist philosophy but was aimed at the Shah and his mentors. But because there was a real likelihood of leftist leadership taking over the reins of revolution from Khomeini, he had to fight on three fronts simultaneously. After toppling the Shah, he not only undertook to eradicate and exterminate all supporters of the former Shah, but also to root out American influcence wherever it was suspected to be. That in itself could have lent support to the leftist ideology which, if permitted to flourish unchecked, might have succeeded in snatching the power from Khomeini's hands and replacing the Islamic ideology with Marx-ism-Leninism.

Fortunately for Ayatollah Khomeini, he was shrewd and powerful enough to wield the double-edged sword of Islamic ideology not only against American rightism but as effectively against Russian leftism.

But when all is said and done, it is clear that, whatever else it was, it certainly was not Islam which guided and instructed the Iranian revolution. At best, you can, if you wish, call what happened and is happening in Iran Khomeinism. The real forces at work are not truly and essentially religious in character. Political powers have exploited the reaction of the Iranians against the Shah to achieve purely political ends.

There is a long history of a growing Iranian consciousness of its exploitation and enslavement by foreign powers of one type or another. Despite the fact that a very large majority of Iranians are Muslims, one cannot ignore the fact that Iranians have never been able to forget or forgive the conquest by Arabs of their homelands. Although the wounds appeared to have been healed long ago and many potent factors such as commonality of religion and common enmity against other countries have played an important role in cementing the Iranians to the Arabs, it cannot be denied that there is still an undercurrent of dissatisfaction at the Arab domination of Iran for the past few centuries. One must also bear in mind that in the pre-Islamic era, Iran could boast one of the most powerful and illustrious civilisations ever to have influenced mankind anywhere in the world. At the inception of Islam, the Arabs knew of only two worlds - that in the West, dominated by the Roman Empire, and that in the East, commanded and governed by the Chosroes of Iran. The memories of that remote and glorious past, though subdued to some extent by the strong influence of Islamic brotherhood, could not entirely be wiped out. There always has been a long and lingering shadow of the great Iranian civilization in the hearts of Iranian intellectuals.

The long history of Iranian-Arab feuds and Iranian punitive excursions into Arabia also left ugly and irritating scars on the Arab minds which even the great healer, time, could not obliterate. This is only human. People throughout the world may sometimes find it difficult to dissociate themselves from the past or to forget injuries and insults to their honour. Such chapters of history are never permanently closed but are opened again and again.

Enough of Arab-Iranian feuds of the past. Let us now turn to more modern times. It is not against the Arabs alone that the Iranians have been nursing their grievances. During the Second World War, the Iranians were subjected to a worse kind of domination by predominantly British forces. Whilst in the Arab case there had at least been the redeeming factor of a common cultural and religious bond, in the case of the British the chasm between the ruler and the ruled, rather than narrowing, grew wider. Nor could it be bridged by any social, cultural or religious similarities.

After the decline of British influence there followed an era of indirect control and subjugation of Third World countries by the major powers through stooges and puppet regimes. It was in this period of neo-imperialism that the Iranian protégé was transferred from the British lap to the American lap. The Shah of Iran thus became a symbol of American imperialism which supported conflicting ideologies to its own as it does today, for example, in Poland, Nicaragua, Israel and South Africa.

The fuel of hatred which was ultimately sparked off by the Khomein-ian revolution was not only a product of American oppression but had been accumulating for centuries, like the subterranean reserves of oil and gas. The important point to note is that this hatred was not essentially religious in origin. If Khomeini had not exploited the hatred in the name of Islam, some communist leader would certainly have exploited it in the name of social justice. Whatever religious or irreligious name was given to the revolution, the underlying forces and factors would remain the same.

I have pointed out many times to those who regard excesses commit-ted by Khomeini against some of his own people, and acts of revenge perpetrated in other countries, as Islamic in character that Islam as a religion has nothing to do with the expression of Iranian dissatisfaction. In a manner of speaking, the West should treat Ayatollah Khomeini as their benefactor rather than as their enemy. I say this because I am quite postive that if Khomeini had not exploited the situation and given it an Islamic face in order to support and perpetuate a junta of Muslim 'clergy', the situation would most certainly have been exploited by Iranian leaders of leftist inclination. The same Iran which we see as green sprinkled with red today would have instead appeared to us entirely red. It would be naïve to say that the communist leadership created and trained by Dr Mossadeq had been weakened and enfeebled to such a degree at the time of the Shah's overthrow that it could not have played an effective and revolutionary role at this epoch-making juncture of Iranian history. In fact, the communist leadership was well supported and trained. It was entirely ready to seize an opportunity. But for Ayatollah Khomeini, Iran could well have ended up as a radical Marxist regime. Such an event would have had disastrous consequences for the oil-rich but militarily weak Middle East. So even Khomeinian Islam - however gory and loathsome it may appear to the West - could be seen as a blessing in disguise. The role of Ayatollah Khomeini should be seen in this perspec-tive.

The Iraq-Iran war may not appear to be relevant to the subject under discussion but it does throw some light on the nature of explosive events in a part of the world of Islam. Both countries claim to be Muslim and purport to draw their inspiration for hating, destroying, and annihilating each other from the sacred name of Islam.

All the soldiers who died in the battle on the Iraqi side were applauded as great martyrs by the Iraqi media. All the Iranian soldiers who died at the hands of the Iraqis were condemned as infidels despatched straight to hell by the Iraqi media. Exactly the same story was repeated in reverse day in and day out on the other side of the border in Iran. Whenever an Iraqi soldier was bayoneted to death the battlefield resounded with the cry of 'Allaho Akbar' (God is the greatest). On which side was Islam? One wonders! All this demonstrates the hollowness of these slogans. The only point which can be proved beyond a shadow of doubt is that the Iraqi and Iranian soldiers who laid down their lives for an apparently noble cause were duped by their leadership. Islam was neither here nor there.

The Holy Quran states:

Allah will surely defend those who believe, Allah loves not the perfidious and the ungrateful. Permission to fight is granted to those against whom war is made, because they have been wronged, and Allah indeed has the power to help them. They are those who have been driven out of their homes unjustly only because they affirmed: our Lord is Allah. If Allah did not repel the aggression of some people by means of others, cloisters and churches and synagogues and mosques, wherein the name of Allah is oft commemorated, would surely be destroyed. Allah will surely help him who helps His cause; Allah is indeed Powerful, Mighty. (22.39-41)

Whenever they kindle a fire to start a war, Allah puts it out. They strive to create disorder in the land and Allah loves not those who create disorder. (5.65)

If two parties of believers should fall out with each other and start fighting, make peace between them. If one of them should transgress against the other, fight the one that transgresses until it submits to the command of Allah. Then if it should so submit, make peace between them with equity, and act justly. All believers are brothers; so make peace between your brothers, and be mindful of your duty to Allah that you may be shown mercy. (49.10-11)

During the war, the above teachings were ignored by the warring nations. In Mecca during the times of the annual pilgrimages some attempts were made by Iran to deliver the message of Khomenian revolution to the rest of the Muslim world through the pilgrims who came there. Unfortunately, these attempts sometimes resulted in very ugly situations, to the extreme embarrassment of Muslims. For instance, what happened in Mecca during the 1987 pilgrimage and the extreme counter-measures taken by Saudi Arabia were much talked about in the Western media. The Holy Quran, however, teaches all Muslims: 'But fight them not in the proximity of the Sacred Mosque unless they fight you therein, should they fight you even there, then fight them; such is the requital of disbelievers.' (2.192)

One benefit which all the great powers (which have overtly or covertly been supporting Israel), chief among them being the USA, have drawn from Khomeini and Khomeinism is that Khomeini was left with no choice but to prolong the Iraq-Iran war. That diverted the attention of the Muslim world from a most irritating thorn in their side, Israel, towards a completely different issue. The consciousness of an external enemy threat gave way to a growing mistrust between one Muslim and another.

The Middle Eastern world was torn apart. The 'fear' of Israel was shelved as a minor and latent danger which could be attended to later. The fear of one section of Muslims for another was a far more pressing and demanding factor which put into oblivion real or imaginary fears about an external enemy. Of course, to dupe the simple common soldier, the slogan that Islam was in danger was often used on both sides. In reality, what was happening was the revival of historic rivalries and jealousies between the Arabs and the Iranian *ajm* (non-Arabs, aliens). It was not a question of Islamic versus non-Islamic forces or Shiaism versus Sunnism, but a simple and straightforward re-enactment of feuds surviving over thousands of years. That is why even those Arabs who had formerly been critical of Iraq and Saudi Arabia were inevitably led to taking the side of Iraq. It was simply a matter of Arab survival against the growing challenge and threat from Iran.

The Arabs indulged in prolonged inter-tribal feuds over petty matters before the advent of Islam. Islam put a stop to this. It joined Muslims into a brotherhood, free of rivalries and discrimination of any sort. But when Muslims ceased to live by the teachings of Islam, brothers became foes and tribal rivalries returned to the forefront. So what we observe in the world of Islam is not truly Islamic in character. It is another case of the revival of old feudalistic tendencies.

The great powers roundly condemned the war and repeatedly demanded a cessation of hostilities, but they were themselves responsible for a constant supply of arms to both Iraq and Iran. After all, warplanes, rockets, missiles, cannons, tanks, other artillery vehicles and destructive weapons which were freely used by both warring factions were not manufactured on their own soils. Overtly and covertly, Middle Eastern oil and Western weapons changed hands. The fire of war was fuelled, in the ultimate analysis, by the oil which was produced by Iraq and Iran and converted into weapons by Western and Eastern non-Muslim powers. As far as the West was concerned, this was not a bad bargain at all - Middle Eastern oil was bought in exchange for obsolete or relatively old weapons. What more advantageous bargain could be envisaged than this?

As we have seen, even the Israeli arch-enemy was totally forgotton. Muslims killed Muslims. The oil of the Muslim world was used to burn and destroy the economy of the Muslim world. The painstaking economic achievements of the previous decade were nullified. As far as progress and prosperity were concerned, instead of moving forwards both Iraq and Iran started to travel backwards in time.

Of course, all wars have devastating effects on economic development, material and human resources, cultural achievements and industry. But in the case of advanced countries, the war industry can be supported from their own resources or those of their allies. The demands and pressures of war and the struggle for survival do not simply drain their resources; it enriches their scientific knowledge and technical know-how to a remarkable degree in a short span of time. The knowledge and expertise gained during times of war can be employed immediately afterwards not just to rehabilitate the economy but to give it a tremendous boost. The destructive wars give rise to new constructive ideas and breakthroughs in scientific and industrial achievements. Therefore, though impoverished materially as a result of a prolonged war, they can be greatly enriched in order to build a better future.

Such, alas, is not the case in the scientifically and economically backward countries which indulge in the luxury of war. Their only choice is to sell whatever they have and even pawn their future by making arrangements with scientifically and industrially advanced countries to supply them with war materials. Without doing that, it would be impossible for any war in the Third World to be prolonged for such a long time and with such devastating effect, as happened in the Iraq - Iran war. The responsibility for whatever attrocities these countries commit against each other and occasionally against other countries must, to some extent, be shared by those who are responsible for the supply of arms and ammunition to them.

When all has been said and done, all debts settled, and the exchange of commodities taken into account, perhaps it would be pertinent to consider the question of who after all is the beneficiary of the hostilities?

We have seen that Islam is condemned as a barbaric religion which upholds terrorism, preaches hatred and intolerance and divides adherents into opposing camps of bloodthirsty foes. This is not surprising. There are fringe benefits to be obtained by those who design, plot, implement and provide the instruments of destruction to the most unfortunate warring factions of the Muslim *umma*.

Incidentally, the term 'Islamic terrorism' leads to another interesting term which has been coined by the Western media in the last decade: 'Islamic nuclear bomb'. Pakistan is alleged to possess this. Of course, there has to be an Islamic nuclear bomb if there is any such thing as Islamic terrorism. Maybe some other terms applicable to various modes of war will become attached to the prefix 'Islamic'. Why do we not hear of a Christian nuclear bomb, a Jewish nuclear bomb, a Hindu nuclear bomb, an Apartheid bomb or a Shinto bomb? It is strange that with the possibility of referring to thousands of other 'religions' bombs, the Western media has chosen only to pick upon, identify and censure the single Islamic bomb, whose very existence is doubtful.

As stated earlier, the real forces at work are not truly and essentially religious in character. Why single out 'Islamic' whenever terrorist forces are at work today in Muslim groups or countries? Those powers responsible for the prolongation of the Iraq-Iran war by ensuring a constant supply of arms cannot escape their responsibility for the immense waste of life and property and the indescribable human suffering that has resulted from it. Whatever their ulterior motives may have been, they will only help Khomeinism to survive longer. Had the warring countries been left alone with their meagre resources, Khomeinism might have started to decline.

Among other things, this war revived and strengthened a nationalist spirit which diverted the attention of the Iranians from internal problems towards the threat of an external enemy. It would be surprising had more disillusionment not arisen within Iran, possibly resulting in an open challenge to and even rebellion against Khomeinism. Within Iran, there is a very strong tendency towards assessing the values of the revolution and judging its pros and cons. Though a major part of the élite has been wiped out, the intellectuals who have survived are bound to reassess their losses and gains during the Khomeinian revolution. A move towards finding a new order for Iran could be imminent.

During the war, the need to keep up the morale of the common masses in Iran was amply met by the excitement of the conflict. When Iran runs out of morale, that will be the day of great uncertainty. Whether the present regime is replaced by leftist or rightist forces or by whatever is left of the middle-roaders, there will certainly be a great battle to gain supremacy and take over the government. Everything will go back into the melting-pot and nobody can say for certain what is in store for Iran. Allah knows best. I can only pray for the people of Iran that their difficult times may come to a peaceful and happy conclusion. They are a brave and gifted people indeed. They have suffered so much in the past and are still suffering, both at the hands of non-Iranian and Iranians - and, ironically, they have also acquired a bad name into the bargain. May Allah show mercy upon them and deliver them from their great predicament.

Now we turn to another aspect of the Khomeinian revolution in Iran. Soon after coming to power, Ayatollah Khomeini planned not only to change the life-style of Iranian Muslims from overt or covert foreign domination, but he also committed himself to bring about similar revolutions in the neighbouring Muslim states. He also made it known to the Muslim world that he would play a stronger role in helping the Palestinians and defeating the Zionist forces. Obviously, neither the other Muslim states nor the state of Israel were willing to receive couriers of the Iranian revolution with open arms, so the export could not be effected through legal and peaceful means. Iran has failed to deliver the revolutionary goods to neighbouring Muslim countries. It has achieved a measure of success, without doubt, in the Palestinian - Israeli sector. As I have already explained, the terrorist activities carried out in this area, whether directed against Israel or against representatives of Western powers, take their licence not from Islam but from the philosophy of the Iranian revolution alone.

The growing talk of militancy and the use of force which we hear needs to be carefully analysed before we can understand the importance of this bizarre phenomenon. The narrow, non-tolerant attitude is certainly becoming more popular with the Muslim 'clergy' in almost all Muslim countries. The responsibility for this mainly lies on the shoulders of Saudi Arabia, which is attempting to capture the imagination of the whole Muslim world and seems resolved to spread its political influence under a religious guise. As it enjoys the unique advantage of being the custodian of the two holiest cities in Islam, Mecca and Medina, it is certainly in a position to exploit this situation to its best advantage.

The religious philosophy of the Saudis emanates from Wahabism, which draws its inspiration from the non-tolerant world of medieval Islam rather than from the more understanding and benign Islam of the time of the Holy Prophet[sa]. The spread of Saudi influence is aided by Saudi petro-dollars and the collosal size of Saudi bank balances in major banks throughout the world. It is to the credit of Saudi Arabia that part of the interest accruing from these collosal investments is being used to form channels of aid from Saudi Arabian coffers to the poorer Muslim nations with sizeable Muslim populations. More often than not, this aid is provided not to boost their ailing economies, but to build mosques, training schools and institutes producing scholars of a Saudi brand.

Hence, wherever you follow the flow of Saudi aid, you will also observe a rapid increase in the narrow, non-tolerant attitudes of Muslim 'clergy'. No doubt, when the Christian world hears these voices roundly condemning all non-Islamic values and preaching *jihad* (that is, holy war), against non-Islamic governments, they are led to believe that the talk of this holy war will readily be translated into actual belligerency. What is happening is in fact completely different .

The Muslim 'clergy' talk loudly about holy wars and the utter destruction of non-Islamic forces. What they actually mean by non-Islamic forces is not Christian, Jewish, Buddhist, or atheist forces. According to their view, all Muslim sects other than their own are either non-Muslim in their character or hold to doctrines that render them liable to earn the wrath of Allah and His true servants. The real enemies of Islam, as they discern them, are not non-Muslims but some sects of Islam within the world of Islam. The awakening militant tendencies are much more directed by Muslims of one sect against Muslims of another sect than against non-Muslims. This is why so much stress is laid by them on capital punishment for apostasy. That is their weapon against Muslims who differ on some doctrinal issues from the majority sect of a country. These sects are, in fact, dealt the death blow in two steps - first, their doctrines are declared to be non-Islamic, which earns them the title of apostates; and second, the doctrine of death being the penalty for apostasy, they are considered liable to be executed.

A neutral observer will agree that this growing militant tendency is creating disorder among the Muslims themselves and that it is reponsible for generating extreme hatred in the hearts of adherents of one sect against the adherents of another.

As far as the non-Muslim powers are concerned, they can feel completely safe and should rest assured that there is no danger whatsoever to them from the so-called militant tendencies of the Muslim world. To demonstrate this, one has only to consider the relationship of Saudi Arabia with the West, particularly the USA. It is inconceivable that Saudi Arabia or countries under her influence could even dream of raising the sword against the USA or her allies. The Saudi regime is 100 per cent dependent for survival on the USA. Almost the entire wealth of the ruling family is deposited with American and Western banks. On top of this, the dependence upon the West for internal and external security is so obvious that it need not be dwelt upon here. These two factors alone guarantee that neither Saudi Arabia nor any Muslim country under her influence can ever pose a threat to the non-Muslim West. Moreover, the very fact that none of the Muslim states is today self-reliant in its production of war materials, and has to depend either upon the West or East for all of its defensive or offensive requirements, provides more than enough of a guarantee for the safe and peaceful conduct of their relations with non-Muslim powers. The same principle is applicable to countries like Libya and Syria, which enjoy more cordial relationships with Eastern powers than with Western ones.

No one who has even a remote understanding of modern warfare can imagine a real threat from so-called 'Islamic' militancy. Of course, there is danger in these growing tendencies and one is bound to be perturbed by them. The danger from 'Islamic' militancy is a threat to the world of Islam itself; it is an inward-looking threat which is destroying the peace of Muslims everywhere. All the intolerance, narrow-mindedness and bigotry which we observe in the Muslim world today is playing havoc with the peace of the Muslim world. Alas!

I am conscious of the fact that, strictly speaking, the word 'terrorism' applies to acts of terror, attempts to cause bomb explosions, and so on. But I do not believe that this is the only type of terrorism the world is suffering from. I believe that whenever repressive measures are taken by governments against their own countrymen to still the voice of disagreement, those measures too should be included within the term 'terrorism' and be as strongly and roundly condemned as any other form of terrorism. I consider all oppressive measures taken by governments against the left or right within their own countries as terrorism of the worst type. When acts of terrorism are directed against foreign governments and take the form of the use of explosives here and there, or the hijacking of planes, such events gain a great deal of attention. World opionion sympathises with the victims of such callous terrorist acts, as indeed it should. Such sympathies are not merely voiced, but are generally followed by constructive means to prevent and pre-empt such attempts in the future. However, what about those hundreds of thousands of people suffering under the stern and merciless hands of their own governments? Their cries of anguish are seldom heard outside. Their cries of protest are very often muffled by the application of strict measures of censorship. Even if philanthropic agencies like Amnesty International draw the attention of the world to such cruel acts of perse-cution, torture, and denial of human rights, such events are only mildly condemned, if at all, by world governments. More often than not, these are considered to be internal matters for the countries concerned. Instead of being described as acts of terrorism, they are widely mentioned as government efforts to suppress terrorism in these countries, and to establish peace, law and order.

I am quite convinced that in essence all restrictive and punitive measures taken by a government against its own people to suppress a popular movement or suspected opposition, more often than not, go beyond the limits of genuine legal measures and end up as brutal acts of violence designed to strike terror in the hearts of a dissatisfied section of their own people. Humanity has suffered far more through such acts of State terrorism than through all acts of sabotage or hijacking put together. As far as Islam is concerned, it categorically rejects and condemns every form of terrorism. It does not provide any cover or justificiation for any act of violence, be it committed by an individual, a group or a govern-ment.

There are, of course, regions of restlessness in the Muslim world where groups, organisations, and sometimes even governments, seem to be committed to acts of terrorism, violence and sabotage. Palestine, Lebanon, Libya and Syria are often in the news. In a majority of cases, those concerned happen to be Muslim by faith, but there are exceptions. Amongst Palestinians, for instance, there are many who have pledged themselves to terrorism against Israel, but happen to be Christian by faith. For convenience or through lack of knowledge they are all dubbed by the Western media as Islamic terrorists. In Lebanon, there have been Muslim terrorists and Christian terrorists, and also Israeli agents and soldiers involved at one time or another in terrorist activities which appal human sensitivities. But you will not hear of Jewish or Christian terrorism in relation to what is happening in Lebanon. All acts of violence are put together and wrapped up in the package of 'Islamic terrorism'.

As far as Salman Rushdie is concerned, no sane person with any real knowledge of the Holy Quran can agree with Imam Khomeini that his death sentence is based on any Islamic injunction. There is no such punishment for blasphemy in the Holy Quran or in the Traditions of the Holy Prophet of Islam. Blasphemy against God is mentioned in the Holy Quran in the following words:

And abuse not those whom they call upon besides Allah, lest they, out of spite abuse Allah in their ignorance. (Ch. 6:109)

No authorisation has been granted to any man to inflict any punishment for blasphemy against God.

Blasphemy was committed by Jews against Mary, the mother of Christ[as]. It has been mentioned in the Holy Quran, where it says:

And for their disbelief and for their uttering against Mary a grievous calumny. (Ch. 4:151)

Again no punishment other than by God Himself is prescribed. It is both tragic and deplorable that Imam Khomeini has thus inadvertently maligned Islam rather than defending it, and has caused immense damage to the image of Islam in the free world.

The Imam of the Grand Mosque of Azhar, in Cairo, has already discredited Imam Khomeini's edict, and I am certain that there are also many Shia Muslims who would disagree with Imam Khomeini in this instance.

Despite all this, it would be unjust if one were to ignore the real issue. I feel it is unfair, as some politicians and scholars have done, to condemn Khomeini only rather than Salman Rushdie, who has produced a book whose extreme language is deliberately offensive to the many millions of Muslims throughout the world. Nor is this all. The book has helped to undermine peace between Muslims and Christians and, if one can judge from the comments in some letters to national newspapers, to have unleashed the forces of racial intolerance.

Let it be very clear that I do not justify terrorism of any kind whatsoever, whatever the colour, religion, sentiment or objective the terrorist may claim to represent. Islam is my faith and religion; and Islam does not approve of disorder in any form. Islam is far from teaching terrorism.

What is the religion of the terrorism organised and supported by Col. Qaddafi's oil-dollars, one may ask? What again is the religion of terrorist activities that Syria has been indulging in in the past? Is it Islam? If so, what is the difference between this Islam and scientific socialism? Is it not a fact that the *Green Book* of Col. Qaddafi is only green in colour of its binding? The contents of the book are red through and through.

If the terrorist activities of the Muslim 'fundamentalists' of Iran or Libya are to be dubbed as 'Islamic terrorism', the colour of their Islam would appear to be dark green. How could the concept of Islam be diametrically opposed to itself and how could Islam be 'green' and 'red' at the same time, one wonders? If anything, Libya's terrorism can only be seen as nationalist terrorism in disguise. Incidentally, it reminds one of Fidel Castro of Cuba. He marches far ahead of Col. Qaddafi in his taste for violence and terrorism. Yet one never hears his deeds described as Christian terrorism.

One thing leads to another: the discussion of terrorism conjures up before one's vision various phases of history. Christianity has been purportedly involved in ugly acts of persecution and torture, and some Christian monarchs have indulged in brutal acts of violence and persecution under the misguided notion that they were serving the religion of Christ[as]. During the years of the Black Death, 1348-9, were not many Jews burnt alive in their homes? In the age of the Spanish Inquisition, a long reign of terror prevailed under the guidance and direction of some Christian priests. Numerous helpless women at various times, were put to death because they were said to be witches and there was a distorted notion that this was the Christian way of dealing with witchcraft.

However much these acts were related directly to Christianity, the crimes against humanity were a product of a very dark age when ignorance ruled supreme. When will man begin to understand the difference between the conduct of a person and the teachings of his religion? If one confuses the two and tries to understand religion by studying the conduct of its adherents, many questions arise. The conduct of adherents of every religion varies from country to country, from sect to sect, from age to age, and from person to person.

How very different is the conduct of Jesus'[as] disciples from those in Pinochet's Chile, or in South Africa, who claim to uphold Christian values. Which is to represent Christianity? Are we entitled to describe the First and Second World Wars, in which millions of people lost their lives,[1] as Christian wars against humanity? In the Second World War,

118

Russian losses alone are estimated to have exceeded 6.1 million. Three-quarters of the entire population of Bosnia was wiped out. The loss of property and material are of such magnitude as to be almost impossible to assess.[2] Will this enormity be described as Christianity in action or shall we take our understanding of Christianity from those early Christians who, having been struck on one cheek, turned the other cheek towards the striker, and those who were fed to beasts and burned alive in their homes rather than answer violence with violence? I would much rather choose the latter.

Any act of war in a Muslim country is perceived in the West as the extension of 'Islamic terrorism' but in any other country such an act is seen as a political dispute. Why must such dual standards of justice prevail in this day and age? One really begins to wonder if there is an undercurrent of hatred for Islam beneath the apparently calm surface of Christian civilisation. Is it perhaps a hangover from centuries of Crusades against Muslim powers or is it the old wine of the orientalists' venom against Islam served in new goblets? The idea that Islam was spread by the sword is highly questionable. The wars of Muslim governments should be judged according to the prevailing principles of politics and international relations and not on the basis of religion.

The expression of violence is symptomatic of the many diseases in society. The Muslim world today does not know which way to turn. People find themselves dissatisfied about many things over which they have no control whatsoever. They are dead meat for exploitation by their own corrupt leaders or agents and by stooges of foreign powers. Unfortunately, many leaders in Muslim countries themselves seek sanction from Islam for their acts of violence and oppression, as happened in the time of the late General Zia-ul-Haq of Pakistan. Bloody revolutions are totally alien to the philosophy of Islam and have no place in Islamic countries.

As a man of religion, and head of a spiritual community of followers who have faced a century of persecution, terror and cruelty, I most strongly condemn all acts and forms of terrorism because it is my deeply rooted belief that not only Islam but also no true religion, whatever its name, can sanction violence and the bloodshed of innocent men, women and children in the name of God.

> God is love, God is peace!
> Love can never beget hatred,
>   and peace can never lead to war.

NOTES

Editor's Foreword

1 *Report of the Court of Inquiry Constituted Under Punjab Act II of 1954 to Inquire into the Punjab Disturbances of 1953* (Lahore: Government Printing House, Punjab, 1954), 184. Justice Mr Muhammad Munir (president) and Justice Mr M. R. Kayani (member) constituted the committee. Further references to the report will be shown as *Munir Commission Report*.

Chapter 1

1 See P. Schaff, *Select Library of Nicene and Post-Nicene Fathers*, 1st series, vol. IV (Buffalo, 1887).
2 The proclamation of the Unity of God and the propagation of Islam and the Holy Prophet Muhammad[sa].

Chapter 2

1 Maulana Abul Ala Maududi, the *amir* (head) of Jamaati Islami until his death, spent his early life in the former princely Indian state of Hyderabad. The young Maududi left school before completing his secondary education because of his father's death. For some time he worked as editor of the *Al-Jamiyat* of Delhi, the newspaper of the Jamiyat Ulamai Hind. In 1927 he resigned his editorship and, having worked so long with the Deoband *ulema*, he decided to devote himself to the study of theology. He was self-taught in theology, Arabic and English. Despite his great learning, immense knowledge and forceful style of Urdu, which has all the ingredients of scholarship, his critics - especially *ulema* of the Deoband and Lucknow schools - say that his lack of training in theological discipline was his great weakness. In 1941 the Maulana founded the Jamaati Islami and assumed its leadership. He criticised the Jamiyat Ulamai Hind for its composite nationalist theory which exposed Muslim India to the grave dangers of religio-cultural absorption into Hinduism, and at the same time assailed Qaid-i-Azam's Muslim nationalism as no less dangerous than Congress nationalism. To him, it made no difference whether the irreligious Muslims of India survived in the form of Pakistan or not (*Musalman aur Maujudah Siyasi Kashmakash*, Pathankot, 1946, 6-7).

2 *Al-Jihad fil Islam*, 137-8.

3 Revd Dr C. G. Pfander, *Mizanul Haq*, 648, 499.

4 Revd Dr C. G. Pfander, *Tatimma Mizanul Haq*.

5 Washington Irving, *Mahomet and His Successors*, 2 vols. (New York: G.P. Putman's Sons, 1868).

6 *Haqiqat-i Jihad* (Lahore: Taj Company Ltd, 1964), 64; emphasis added.

7 For details of Dr Pfander's campaign against Islam, see 'The Mohommedan controversy', *The Calcutta Review* (Calcutta, July - December 1845), vol. IV, 420.

8 Sir William Muir, *The Life of Mahomet* (London: Smith Elder & Co., 1859), vol. I, 111.

9 Translated from an Urdu speech by Pandit Shastri at a Gorakhpur (India) meeting, 1928, to commemorate the Prophet's[sa] birth, see *Dunya ka Hadi Ghairon ki Nazar Main*, 57, 61.

10 *Sat Updaish*, Lahore, 7 July 1915; see *Barguzida Rasul Ghairon Main Maqbul*, 12, 13.

11 Prof. Ram Dev, *The Prakash*, see *Burguzida Rasul Ghairon Main Maqbul*, 24.

12 Dr D.W. Leitz, *Asiatic Quarterly Review*, October 1886. Dr Leitz has referred to verses 40 and 41 of chapter 22 of the Quran, *Al-Hajj*. The verses say: 'Permission to fight is granted to those against whom war has been made because they have been wronged. Allah indeed has the power to help them. They are those who have been driven out of their homes because they affirmed that our Lord is Allah. If Allah did not repel the aggression of some by the means of others, then surely cloisters, churches, synagogues and mosques - where His name is honoured - would be destroyed?'

13 *Haqiqat-i-Jihad*, *op.cit.*, 65.

14 *Masala'-i-Qaumiyat* (Pathankot: Maktaba Jamaati Islami, 1947), 105.

15 We seek the protection of Allah from this blasphemous use of language, which only Maulana Maududi could use.

16 W. Thomas Arnold, *The Preaching of Islam: a History of the Propagation of the Muslim Faith*, 2nd ed. (London: Constable and Co. Ltd, 1913), 279-80.

17 *Nawan Hindustan*, Delhi, 17 November 1947.

18 Literally, 'The knower of the psyche of the Prophet', or 'The observer of the Prophet's mind'.

Chapter 3

1 William Hailey, to the government of India, 25 July and 12 August 1927, *Government of India Home Political Proceedings 1927*, 132.

2 *Al-Jihad fi'l Islam*, 93. In the second of the subsequent quotations, the words in square brackets have been added. The Arabic words are: *'an yadin wahum saghirun'*.

3 *Ibid.*, 138.

4 *Ibid.*
5 W. Montgomery Watt, *Muhammad at Medina* (Karachi: Oxford University Press, 1981), 15.
6 Will Durant, *The Story of Civilisation*, 11 vols. (New York: Simon & Schuster, 1950); vol. IV, *The Age of Faith*, 168.
7 *Ibid.*, 157.
8 *Ibid.*
9 'They shall beat their swords into ploughshares and their spears into pruning hooks: nation shall not lift up sword against nation, neither shall they learn war any more.' *The Book of the Prophet Isaiah*, 2:4.
10 Maulana Maududi's original Urdu word is *qalbarani*, literally, 'ploughing'.
11 Maharaja Kishen Perhad Shad was a Persian and Urdu poet and was known for his *Nati-i-Rasul (Hymns honouring the Holy Prophet)*.
12 Harriet Rouken Lynton and Mohini Rajan, *The Days of the Beloved* (Berkeley: University of California Press, 1974), ix. The book describes the life and times of Muhbub Pasha (1869-1911), the sixth Nizam of Hyderabad.)
13 He was born on 25 September 1903 in Aurangabad; Arif Batalwi, *Aik Maududi Das Islam* (Lahore).
14 Mu Inuddin Aqil, *Tahrik-i-Pakistan aur Maulana Maududi*, (Karachi: Khayal-Nau, 1971), 27. Most of the biographical details in this book are taken from Muhammad Yusuf's *Maulana Maududi Apni aur Dusron ki Nazar Main* (Lahore: Maktaba Al-Habib, n.d.).
15 Muhammad Yusuf, *op.cit.*, 363-4; and Mu Inuddin Aqil, *op.cit.*, 27.
16 Maulana Maududi had earlier written a book on Gandhiji's biography but it was banned before its publication. Arif Batalvi, *Aik Maududi Das Islam, op.cit.*, 10; see Mumtaz Ali Asi, *Maulana Maududi aur Jamaati Islam, Aik Jaizah*.
17 Mu Inuddin Aqil, *op.cit.*, 26; *see* Muhammad Yusuf, *op.cit.*, 362-3.
18 *Deccan ki Siyasi Tarikh* and *Daulat-i-Asifiyah aur Hukumat-i-Bartaniya*.
19 Fazlur Rahman, *Islam and Modernity - Transformation of an Intellectual Tradition* (Chicago: University of Chicago Press, 1982), 116; emphasis added.
20 *Maktube-i-Hidayat* (Deoband: Kutub Khana Izaziyah), 21; *see* Maulana Muhammad Akhtar, *Maududi Sahib Akabir-i-Ummat-ki Nazar Main* (Bombay).
21 Maulana Muhammad Akhtar, *Maududi Sahib Akabir-i-Ummat-ki Nazar Main, op.cit.*, 9.
22 *ibid.*, 15.
23 *ibid.*, 48.
24 Will Durant, *The Age of Faith, op.cit.*, 159.
25 Joel Carmichael, *The Shaping of the Arabs, a Study In Ethnic Identity* (New York, 1967), 38.
26 Maxime Rodinson, *Mohammed*, trans. Anne Carter (New York, 1971), 194.

Notes

27 The word used by Asma is much more abusive.

28 Two Yemenite tribes.

29 Ibn Hisham, *Kitab Sirat Rasul Allah*, ed. F. Wüstenfeld, 2 vols. (Göttingen, 1856-60), 995-6.

30 The two Ansar tribes, the Aws and Khazraj.

31 Ibn Hisham, *op.cit.*, 995. The translation is by Anne Carter, in Maxime Rodinson, *Mohammed*, *op.cit.*, 157. Like 'Pharaoh' (Egypt) and 'Caesar' (Rome), 'Tubba' was the name given to the ancient kings of south Arabia.

32 Kab's mother belonged to the Jewish tribe an-Nadir. Though his father was an Arab, he was accepted as a member of Banu an-Nadir.

33 Ibn Hisham, *op.cit.*, 548-9; trans. A. Guillaume, *The Life of Muhammad* (London: Oxford University Press, 1970).

34 As the result of a dream, the Holy Prophet decided to go on *umrah* (pilgrimage) to Mecca with 1400 to 1600 men. He camped at the edge of the sacred territory of Mecca, at Al-Hudaybiyah, where envoys between Muslims and Meccans came and went. Finally, a truce was signed, forcing the Muslims to retreat that year on condition that they would be allowed to return to Mecca for *hajj* the following year.

35 The battle of Ahzab or the Trench on 30 March 627.

36 W. Montgomery Watt, *Muhammad at Medina*, *op.cit.*, 69.

37 *ibid.*, 51-2.

38 See p. 22 above.

39 W. Montgomery Watt, *Muhammad at Medina*, *op.cit.*, 4.

40 *ibid.*

41 Martin Lings, *Muhammad, his Life Based on the Earliest Sources* (London: George Allen & Unwin, 1983), 297.

42 Washington Irving, *Mahomet and His Successors*, 2 vols. (New York: G.P. Putman's Sons, 1868), vol. 1, 253.

43 W. Montgomery Watt, *Muhammad at Medina*, *op.cit.*, 68. The valley of Jiranah is about ten miles from Mecca and the spoils of the battle of Hunayn were sent there to be stored.

44 Maxime Rodinson, *Mohammed*, *op.cit.*, 262.

45 Stanley Lane-Poole, *Selections from the Quran and Hadith*, (Lahore: Sind Sagar Academy, n.d.), 28.

46 Maxime Rodinson, *Mohammed*, *op.cit.*, 312.

Chapter 4

1 Maulana Maududi, *Haqiqat-i-Jihad* (Lahore: Taj Company Ltd, 1964), 58.

2 Edward Gibbon, *Decline and Fall of the Roman Empire*, vol. 5, ed. J.B. Buey (London: 1909-14), 332.

3 Bernard Lewis, *The Jews of Islam* (Princeton: Princeton University Press, 1983), 3.

4 James Drever, *A Dictionary of Psychology*, revised by Harvey Wallerstein (1964), 191.

5 Pierre Janet, *Les Observations et la psychasthenie* (Paris: Alcan, 1903); *see* Robert S. Woodsworth and Mary Sheehan, *Contemporary School of Psychology* (New York: The Ronald Press Company, 3rd ed., 1964), 253.

6 Elton Mayo, *Some Notes on the Psychology of Pierre Janet* (Cambridge, Massachusetts: Harvard University Press, 1948); *see* Robert S. Woodsworth and Mary Sheehan, *op.cit.*, 253.

7 Kurt Lewin, 'The Conceptual representation and the measurement of psychological forces', *Contributions to Psychological Theory*, 1, (4), 2.

8 Robert S. Woodsworth and Mary Sheehan, *op.cit.*, 241.

9 The conversion of religion is called *irtidad* and treated as apostasy by Maulana Maududi.

10 Hugh Nissenden, 'Scripture and Survival', *The New York Times Book Review*, 17 March 1985, 12.

11 The Maulana's original Urdu word for 'political power' is *iqtidar*.

12 *Haqiqat-i-Jihad*, *op.cit.*, 10.

13 *ibid.*, 11.

14 *ibid.*, 58.

15 *ibid.*

16 *ibid.*, 16-17.

17 *ibid.* The original Urdu sentence is involved and the Maulana has used the Urdu word *hukumat* twice in the sentence in two different meanings.

18 *ibid.*, 15.

Chapter 5

1 Maulana Abul Ala Maududi, *Murtadd ki saza Islami qanun main*, (Lahore: Islamic Publications Ltd, 1981 8th ed.), 32.

2 Dr Israr Ahmad, *Islam aur Pakistan, Tarikhi siyasi ilmi aur thaqafati pas manzar* (Lahore: Anjuman Khuddam-ul-Quran, 1983), 72. Dr Ahmad is the former chief (Nazim-i-Ala) of the Jamaati Islami student organisation and, later, the Amir of Jamaati Islami Montgomery. He is also the author of *Tahrik-i Jamaati Islami - a Research Paper*. Dr Ahmad resigned from the membership of Jamaati Islami after ten years of involvement in various capacities.

3 The Deoband seminary (*Dar-al-ulum*) was founded in 1867. Deoband is a small town near Delhi.

4 S.G.F. Brandon, *Dictionary of the History of Ideas* (New York, 1973), vol. 11, 342.

5 C. J. Hefele, *History of the Christian Councils* (Edinburgh, (1894), vol. III, 12; *see also* Durant, Will, *The History of Civilisation* (New York, 1950), vol. IV, 48.

Notes

6 Will Durant, *The Story of Civilisation*, 48.

7 P. Schaff, *Select Library of Nicene and Post-Nicene Fathers*, 1st series (Buffalo, 1887), vol. IV, 640.

8 J.E.E. Dalberg-Acton (1st Baron Acton), *The History of Freedom and Other Essays* (London: Macmillan, 1907), 163.

9 *ibid.*, 178-9.

10 Thomas Hobbes, *Leviathan, or Matter, Form and Power of a Commonwealth Ecclesiastical and Civil* (Chicago: Great Books of the Western World, Encyclopaedia Britannica Inc., 1952).

11 *ibid.*, 210.

12 Dr Israr Ahmad, *Islam aur Pakistan*, *op.cit.*, 72.

13 I. Goldziher, *Vorlesungen uber den Islam*, 2nd ed. (Heidelberg, 1925), 183-4; *see* Bernard Lewis, *Islam in History: Ideas, Men and Events in the Middle East* (London, 1973), 231.

14 Bernard Lewis, *The Jews of Islam* (Princeton: Princeton University Press, 1983), 53.

15 *The Daily Tasnim*, 15 August 1952, 12; *see also Mizaj Shanasi Rasul*, 372.

16 Maulana Maududi, *Musalman aur maujuda siyasi kashmaksh*, (Pathankot: Maktaba Jamaati Islami, 1941-2), vol. III, 130.

17 *ibid.*, 132.

18 *ibid.*, 166.

19 *Musalman aur maujuda siyasi kashmakash*, *op.cit.*, vol. III, 95.

20 *Ruidad-i Jamaati Islami* (Ichhra, Lahore: Shu'ba Nashr wa Ishaat, Jamaati Islami, 1970), part 1, 16.

21 *Murtadd ki saza Islam main* (1950), 80-1.

22 *Murtadd ki saza Islami qanun main* (8th ed.), *op.cit.*, 72-3.

23 Al-Bukhari, *Kitab al-Jana'iz*.

24 *Dictionary of the History of Ideas* (New York), vol. IV, 116.

25 *Murtadd ki saza Islami qanun main*, 51.

26 *ibid.*, 32.

27 *Murtadd ki saza Islami qanun main*, 35.

28 Quran, 87. 14.

29 *Murtadd ki saza Islami qanun main*, 51.

30 Maududi, *Haqiqat-i Jihad* (Lahore: Taj Company Ltd, 1964), 64; emphasis added.

31 *ibid.*; emphasis added.

Chapter 6

1 *Sahih al-Bukhari, Bab Kitabat al-Iman al-Nas*.

2 *ibid.*, *Kitab al-Salat, Bab Fadl Istaqbal al-Qiblah*.

3 Al-Ghazali, *Faysal al-Tafriqah bayn al-Islam wa'l Zandaqah* (Cairo, 1901),

68; *see* Bernard Lewis, *Islam in History: Ideas, Men and Events in the Middle East* (London, 1973), 232.

4 *Munir Commission Report* (Lahore, 1954), 28.

5 Abdul Malik Ibn Hisham, *Sirat Rasul Allah* ed. F. Wustenfeld, 2 vols. (Göttingen, 1856-60), 984; trans. A. Guillaume, *The Life of Muhammad* (London: Oxford University Press, 1970), p. 667.

6 *Musnand Imam Ahmad Hanbal*, vol. V, 260.

7 *Mufradat al-Quran*.

8 *Quran*, 6.67. *See also* 6.108, 10.109, 17.55, 39.42 and 42.7. The word *wakil* has been explained by Imam Fakhr ud-Din Razi in *Tafsir Kabir* (Cairo, 1308 AH), vol. IV, 62-3 and also Muhammad Abduh in *Tafsir al-Quran al-Shahir bi Tafsir al-Manar*, ed. Muhammad Rashid Rida (Beirut, 1337 AH), vol. VII, 501-3, 662-3.

9 Emphasis added.

10 Abdul Malik Ibn Hisham, *Kitab Sirat Rasul Allah*, *op.cit.*, 927.

11 *ibid.*, 381.

12 *ibid.*, 384.

13 *Sahih al-Bukhari* (Cairo, n.d.), vol. 1, book 3, 28.

14 Ibn Hisham, *op.cit.*, 818.

15 *ibid.*, 819.

16 *ibid.*, 818-19.

17 *ibid.*, 819.

18 *ibid.*

19 *ibid.*, 820.

20 *ibid.*, 468-9.

21 *ibid.*, 819.

22 *ibid.* Al-Zurqani, *Sharah al-Mawahib al-Laduniyah* (Cairo 1325 AH), vol. II, 315; *see* Shair Ali, *Qatli-Murtadd aur Islam* (Amritsar, 1925), 119.

23 Ibn Hisham, *op.cit.*, 728.

24 *ibid.*, 819.

25 *ibid.*

26 Muhammad Idris al Shafii, *Kitab al-Umm*, ed. Muhammad Zahri al Nadjjar (Cairo, n.d.), vol. VIII, 256.

27 Abu Jafar Muhammad ibn Jarir al-Tabari, *Tarikh al-Rasul wa al-Muluk*, ed. M.J. de Goeje (Leiden, 1964), vol. IV, 1874.

28 C.H. Becker, 'The expansion of the Saracens', *The Cambridge Medieval History* (New York: Macmillan, 1913), vol. II, 335.

29 Muhammad Idris al-Shafii, *op.cit.*, 255-6.

30 Abd al-Hamid Hibet-u-Allah ibn al-Hadid, *Sharah Nahj al-Balaghah*, ed. Muhammad Abu al-Fadl Ibrahim (Cairo, 1956 - 64), vol. XIII, 187.

31 C.H. Becker, *op.cit.*, 335.

32 Bernard Lewis, *The Arabs in History* (London, 1958), 51-2.

33 Ashari, *Maqalat*, vol 1, 191.

34 Ibn Hisham, *op.cit.*, 688-9.

35 *Sahih Muslim with Sharah al-Nawawi* (Lahore: 1958, 62), vol. II, 112-13.

36 For various reports with slightly different wording see *Sahih al-Bukhari* and *Sahih Muslim*, 'Kitab al-Iman'.

37 Bernard Lewis, *Islam in History*, *op.cit.*, 233.

38 See Bernard Lewis's detailed analysis of the genesis and evolution of this institution in Islamic history in *Islam in History*, *op.cit.*, 217-36 and also *The Jews of Islam* (Princeton: Princeton University Press, 1984), 53-4.

39 Bernard Lewis, *The Jews of Islam*, *op.cit*, 100.

40 Ignaz Goldziher, *Mohammed and Islam*, trans. Kate Chambers Seelye (New Haven: Yale University Press, 1917), 74, note 3.

41 Bernard Lewis, *The Jews of Islam*, *op.cit.*, 101.

42 Sir Judanath Sarkar, *Short History of Aurangzib* (Calcutta, 1954), 105-6.

43 But Bab (Door of the Spirit) Mirza Ali Muhammad, who proclaimed his prophethood, was executed at Tabriz on 9 July 1850.

44 *Munir Commission Report*, 218, 219.

45 *ibid.*, 219.

Chapter 7

1 The term used for the first four caliphs (successors) after the death of the Holy Prophet[sa], namely Hazrat Abu Bakr, Umar, Uthman and Ali.(Their rule lasted from AD632 to 661).

2 *Commentary: Bahral Muheet*, vol. II, 493.

3 Tabari, vol. IV, 1873; Ibn Khaldun, vol. II, 65; Khamees, vol. II, 237, etc.

4 Tabari, vol. IV, 1849.

5 Khamees, vol. II, 641.

6 Ibn Hijr Al-Asqalani, *Al-Isaba fi Tamyiz-is-Suhaba* (Beirut: Darul Kitab Al-Arabi), vol. 2, 448; Al Imam-Allama Ibn ul-Athir, *Usudul Ghaba fi Marifatui Sahaba* (Beirut: Dar Ahyaultarath Al-Arabi), vol. 4, 3.

7 Ibn Al-Athir Al-Jazri, *Alkamil fil Tarikh* (Beirut: Darul Kutb Al-Almiya), vol. 2, 201-5.

8 Tabari, vol. IV, 1977.

9 Masboot, vol. x, 110.

10 Fateh Al-Bari, vol. XII, 267; Imam Razi, *Tafsir Kabir*, vol. III, 614; Sheikh Ibn Taimiyyah, *Minhajus Sunnah*, vol. II, 61-2; Tarikh-al Kamil, vol. III, 148.

11 Bukhari, *Kitab al-Mustadeen wal Muanadeen wa Qitalihin*, Bab Hukumul Murtad wal Murtadda.

12 Abu Daud.

13 The Holy Quran urges: 'When you heard of it, why did not the believing men and the believing women think well of their own people, and say: This is a manifest lie ... ' (24.13)

The Holy Prophet[sa] said: 'It is evidence enough of the untruthfulness of a person that he should relate, without examining, whatever he hears.' (Muslim, vol. 1, chapter headed 'Don'ts about Tradition')

14 Bukhari Mishkat (Egypt), 9-10; Bukhari and Fateh Al-Bari, *Hadith*, no. 6922 (Egypt), vol. 12, 267.

15 Abdul Hayy, *Al-Rafa wal Takmeel*.

16 Not to be confused with Ikramah b. Abu Jahl.

17 Ibn Saad, *Al Tabqa Al-Kabir*, vol. 2, 386.

18 *Mizan Al-Aitadal*, vol. 2, 208.

19 Abu Daud, vol. II, 35.

20 Abu Jafar Muhammed b. Amr b. Musa b. Hamad Al-Aqbli Al-Mulki, *Kitab al-Soafa Al-Kabir* (Lebanon: Darul Kutb Al-Almiyya). Al Safr III, 1983, 373.

21 Abu Jafar Muhammad b. Amr b. Musa b. Hamad Al-Aqbli Al-Mulki, *op.cit.*

22 *Mizan Al-Aitadal*, vol. 2, 209.

23 *Fateh Al-Bari*.

24 The son of Abbas, an uncle of the Holy Prophet[sa]. Ibn Abbas was no more than a child during the Holy Prophet's[sa] time.

25 Bukhari, *Kitab al-Janaiz*, chapter headed 'Wailing Over the Dead'.

26 *Hedayah*.

27 *Fateh al-Kadeer*, vol IV, 389; vol II, 580.

28 Chalpi, *Commentary on Fateh al-Kadeer*, 388; *Inayah*, 390.

Chapter 8

1 *Munir Commission Report*, 258.

2 Maxime Rodinson, *Mohammad*, trans. Anne Carter (New York, 1971), 194. 'A tribal poet among the Bedouin,' as Joel Carmichael puts it, was 'no mere versifier, but a kindler of battle', his poems were 'thought of as the serious beginning of real warfare' (*The Shaping of the Arabs, a Study in Ethnic Identity*, New York, 1967, 38).

3 Ibn Hisham, *Kitab Sirat Rasul Allah*, 995. The English translation is by Anne Carter, given in Rodinson's *Mohammed*, *op.cit.*, 157.

4 Ali b. Burhan ud Din ud-Halabi, *Insan al-Uyun*, vol. II, 116; cited by Kister, *The Journal of the Economic and Social History of the Orient*, vol. VIII, 267.

5 Ibn Hisham, *op.cit.*, 459.

6 Ibn Hisham, *op.cit.*, 550, this translation by A. Guillaume.

7 *ibid.*, 386.

8 *ibid.*

9 *ibid.*, 387.

10 *ibid.*, 726.

11 *ibid.*

Notes

12 *ibid.*

13 Will Durant, *The Story of Civilisation*, 11 vols. (New York: Simon & Shuster, 1950), vol. IV, *The Age of Faith*, 301.

14 *Munir Commission Report*, 259.

15 In the subcontinent they are generally known as Brelvis.

16 *Deobandi Maulwiyon ka Iman* (Lyallpur: Shahi Masjid, n.d.).

17 *Razakhani Fitna Pardazon ka siyah jhoot.*

18 Shah Muhammad Asi and Syed Muhammad Tanha, *Shourish' urf Bhare ka Tattoo*, 7-8.

19 Wilfred Cantwell Smith, *Modern Islam in India* (Lahore, 2nd ed., 1947).

20 *Munir Commission Report*, 257.

21 Mirza Ghulam Ahmad, *Izala-i Awham* (Amritsar, 1891), part 1, 176.

22 Mirza Ghulam Ahmad, *A'ina-i-Kamalat* (Qadian, 1893), last page.

23 *ibid.*

24 Mirza Ghulam Ahmad, *op.cit., Izala-i-Awham*, 138.

25 Mirza Ghulam Ahmad, *Tawdih-i-Maram* (Amritsar, 1308 AH), 23.

26 According to the Quran, Abraham's[as] father's name was Azar, (Adhar) the name given by the Church historian, Eusebius, and not Terah as given in Genesis 11:26; Quran, 6.75.

27 Sir Muhammad Iqbal, *Bang-i-Dara*, *Jawab-i-Shikwah*, stanzas VII, IX, X and XVII, trans. A. J. Arberry.

28 Aziz Ahmad and G.E. Grunebaum (eds.) *Muslim Self-Statement in India and Pakistan, 1857 - 1968* (Wiesbaden, 1970), 13.

Chapter 9

1 In the First World War, the mobilised forces of the Allies totalled 42.6 million and the Central Powers had 22.85 million. Total casualties on both sides were 57.6 per cent. In the Second World War, the peak armed strength was 72,581,566, out of which 16,829,758 were killed or missing (presumed killed) and 26,698,339 were wounded. (Source: Arthur Guy Enock, *This War Business*, London: Bodley Head, 1951, and US Department of Defence.) The Carnegie Endowment for International Peace has estimated that the First World War cost $400,000,000,000, excluding civilian property damage and the cost of loss of life. According to one estimate, the direct costs of the Second World War for the participating nations were a staggering grand total of $1,098,938,000,000.

2 William J. Roehrenbeck, *Collins Encyclopaedia*, vol. 23, article headed 'War Costs and Casualties'.